SEEDS OF LIGHT, SEEDS OF JOY

Growing with God in Everyday Life

To JoAnne,

Blessings!

Sara Ray

S A R A   R A Y

WESTBOW
PRESS®
A DIVISION OF THOMAS NELSON
& ZONDERVAN

Scripture quotations taken from the New American Standard Bible®, Copyright © 1960, 1962, 1963, 1968, 1971, 1972, 1973, 1975, 1977, 1995 by The Lockman Foundation. Used by permission. (www.Lockman.org)

Scripture taken from the Holy Bible, NEW INTERNATIONAL VERSION®. Copyright © 1973, 1978, 1984 by Biblica, Inc. All rights reserved worldwide. Used by permission. NEW INTERNATIONAL VERSION® and NIV® are registered trademarks of Biblica, Inc. Use of either trademark for the offering of goods or services requires the prior written consent of Biblica US, Inc.

Scripture taken from the New Century Version. Copyright © 2005 by Thomas Nelson, Inc. Used by permission. All rights reserved.

Scripture taken from the Holman Christian Standard Bible ® Copyright © 2003, 2002, 2000, 1999 by Holman Bible Publishers. All rights reserved.

Revised Standard Version of the Bible, copyright ©1952 [2nd edition, 1971] by the Division of Christian Education of the National Council of the Churches of Christ in the United States of America. Used by permission. All rights reserved.

Scripture taken from the New King James Version. Copyright © 1979, 1980, 1982 by Thomas Nelson, Inc. Used by permission. All rights reserved.

This book is a work of non-fiction. Unless otherwise noted, the author and the publisher make no explicit guarantees as to the accuracy of the information contained in this book and in some cases, names of people and places have been altered to protect their privacy.

WestBow Press books may be ordered through booksellers or by contacting:

WestBow Press
A Division of Thomas Nelson & Zondervan
1663 Liberty Drive
Bloomington, IN 47403
www.westbowpress.com
1 (866) 928-1240

Because of the dynamic nature of the Internet, any web addresses or links contained in this book may have changed since publication and may no longer be valid. The views expressed in this work are solely those of the author and do not necessarily reflect the views of the publisher, and the publisher hereby disclaims any responsibility for them.

Any people depicted in stock imagery provided by Thinkstock are models, and such images are being used for illustrative purposes only. Certain stock imagery © Thinkstock.

ISBN: 978-1-5127-1852-2 (sc)
ISBN: 978-1-5127-1853-9 (hc)
ISBN: 978-1-5127-1851-5 (e)

Library of Congress Control Number: 2015918303

Print information available on the last page.

WestBow Press rev. date: 11/12/2015

For Bob

Thank you for choosing me,
for encouraging me,
for loving me …
I look forward to seeing you again
when we meet in Heaven.

CONTENTS

PREFACE

This book has been "in the works" for quite some time. It began one Sunday in 1999 during Communion time. I was sitting in church meditating on the sacrifice of Jesus when a story application popped into my head. Along with it came an "impression" that I needed to write devotions and send them out via email. I tried to ignore it, but just like other things the Lord encouraged me to do, the strong feeling I had would not go away.

At home, I wrote down the words to the application that had permeated my thinking during Communion. I composed an email that explained what I was doing and why, added my devotion, and sent it to several people. After the initial "mailing", I began to write more and more; sending out devotions almost every day. I have to admit that I was astonished at the results.

Several people that I emailed forwarded the devotions to others, who forwarded them to still others. Some of the ones that had received forwards contacted me directly and asked me to add them to my list. I also heard from people who wanted to let me know how much a particular devotion meant to them. It was then that the encouragement to put my devotions into a book began to take place.

I wrote devotions daily for a while, but then my family moved to the country and I did not have as much time to sit and write every morning. However, I composed a lot of them in my head as I was doing other tasks. I emailed devotions on a much more sporadic basis and then stopped altogether. Then I started to hear from people who missed my devotions, wanting to know when I was going to start sending them again. All the while, I was still receiving encouragement to put my devotions into book form.

A few years ago, I started reading through some of the devotions I had written. At the time, I made up a new list of recipients and started sending them out again; a few new ones intermingled with several I "recycled". And still the suggestions came – "You need to put these into a book!"

In the meantime, I had followed another path with my writing as well; I began authoring the "Cooks' Corner" column for our local newspaper. I was to provide recipes and stories once a week. I have recently completed my ninth year of writing for the newspaper. Now I have two requests from people – the first is for a book of devotions and the second for a cookbook!

My husband was strongly in favor of me doing both; however, he developed multiple myeloma (a blood plasma cancer) in 2009. I spent a lot of time after that dealing with all his medical issues and taking care of his needs. When he finally lost his battle to that horrible disease in October of 2012, I was in no frame of mind to put together a book.

Sometimes it seems like the Lord knocks us in the head and says, "Do it now!" That is what happened to me this past summer. I have chosen 120 of my devotions and prepared them for publication. It is my hope that all the people who have been requesting a book of my devotions will be pleased that I finally managed to provide one for them.

ACKNOWLEDGEMENT

First and foremost, I want to acknowledge the Holy Spirit of God and thank Him for all the inspiration He has provided me. Without His guidance and direction, this book would not have been written.

Secondly, I need to acknowledge my late husband, Bob Ray. He provided me with so much encouragement and affirmation. He had confidence in me even when I had no confidence in myself. He loved being my "critic"; I often had him check my writing for awkward spots, spelling errors, and other mistakes. I know he would have been excited about this book!

My family comes next; not only have they supported my writing, but they have also supplied a lot of story material as well! My family includes my children and their spouses, my grandchildren, and my siblings, along with a special cousin who might as well be a sibling. I would also be remiss in not mentioning my parents, now in Heaven, who first taught me about Jesus.

Lastly, I have to thank each and every person who has encouraged me to put my devotions into book form. It has been a long time coming, but I finally took your advice!

INTRODUCTION

"Light is sown like seed for the righteous, and gladness for the upright in heart" (Psalm 97:11a NASB).

Each time I read through the Psalms during the past few years, this verse seemed to jump off the page at me. Then it began shouting to me until I could no longer ignore the words that kept building up inside me.

I used to carry and read the New International Version of the Bible (NIV), but now I use the New American Standard Bible (NASB). It is a personal preference of mine; the translation is word by word instead of thought by thought, and I often get a clearer picture of what the Lord is trying to tell me. When I looked this verse up in the NIV, I found out that the words "like seed" were not there. And to me, those two words give a whole lot of meaning to the verse. They are the ones that set my thoughts in motion.

The picture of light and gladness being sown like seed is what has so intrigued me. I picture the Lord with a seed bag over His shoulder walking through the fields of life. He reaches into the bag and tosses out handfuls of glittering "light seeds"–seeds that sparkle like diamonds in the sun. Laughing joyfully, He reaches in for another handful of seed; however, this time He draws out seeds of gladness–tiny iridescent bubbles of joy–and strews them among the light seeds. He keeps walking and planting, never running out of seed and never growing weary from His labor. His face is full of delight, and He chuckles as He thinks of the blessings His children will receive as the seeds grow in their lives.

As I pondered this picture, I thought of the Jesus' parable of the sower in Luke 8. I began to wonder if seeds of light and gladness fall in places where they will never grow to their full potential. I became convicted by the reminder that there are times when I intentionally keep them from sprouting in my life. Now the picture changes from joy and light to frustration with myself. But that frustration, when followed by conviction, can be the means by which I open myself to the Lord and allow the seeds to grow.

I want to be the fertile ground Jesus refers to in His parable. I so desire the light "seeds" and joy "seeds" to grow in my life. God has given me times of joy and light during the dark days I find myself traveling through since cancer claimed the life of my husband. I am very thankful that He has given me the ability to realize He is still planting seeds to grow in my life. Now it is time for me to let them! For each of you reading this, my prayer is that you will allow them to grow in your life, too.

When the Lord first brought this verse (Psalm 97:11) to my attention, I had the idea of writing a book of devotions about joy and light. However, this would require a lot more effort than compiling devotions I had already written. My tendency to procrastinate or to find myself too "busy" would snuff out the good intention to write. I did what I very often do when faced with a dilemma – took it to the Lord. He gently reminded me that the light and joy "seeds" were scattered among everyday life.

We all have times when we need light; we need the Lord to open our eyes to see His truth and to let it overcome the darkness of the world around us. We have times we need to be admonished to do the right thing, and we also need to find encouragement to be overcomers. Sometimes we are in dire need of a good dose of pure and unmitigated joy. Life can be so very hard. A season of laughter works wonders when it comes to refreshing our spirits – it helps us be better able to go on with living.

I am thankful to the Lord that He gave me the ability to find light and understanding in the middle of everyday things. He has taught me so much using the world around me as His instructor. I am blessed to find His joy surrounding me as well. It still amazes me how He can provide times of rejoicing during my most difficult days.

This book of devotions is full of things I have learned from what could be considered some unusual sources. It also has moments of humor. Sometimes they come with a lesson and sometimes they are meant to be nothing more than a source of amusement which hopefully brings a smile to your face and laughter to your soul.

It is my sincerest wish that through my experiences, you will discover ways that the Lord can speak into your life; that you, too, can learn to grow Seeds of Light and Seeds of Joy.

Day 1

AS THE SUN COMES UP

My morning time of prayer was put on hold one day because I was outside with my camera taking pictures of the sun coming up. The colors of the sunrise beckoned me to go outdoors and enjoy a time of watching our Creator at work. Although it was a bit chilly, I kept watching as the sun crept further up in the sky. At first I could not see the sun itself, but its rays of light lit up the clouds preceding its arrival. The clouds reflected the coming glory with brilliant shades of pinks and purples. As the sun climbed higher, those first rays were swallowed up in its overwhelming brightness, becoming one with the huge ball of light that shone through the treetops. I stood there in awe. Even though the sun rises every morning, no two sunrises are ever the same. God set the universe in motion – day follows day, month follows month, and year follows year – yet every day is a new day.

As Christians, we are to anticipate the arrival of God's Son much like the clouds anticipated the arrival of the sun. We should reflect the light and glory of our coming Savior to the world around us. They desperately need to know that there is a Creator God who has provided a way for them to know Him through His Son. When we can take the clouds in our lives (times when we are being tested in some way or other) and allow God to shine His light through our circumstances, we declare to the world that there is a Savior. We should be looking forward to the day when God is the only light we will need.

"And there will no longer be any night; and they will not have need of the light of a lamp nor the light of the sun, because the Lord God will illumine them; and they will reign forever and ever" (Revelation 22:5 NASB).

Day 2

KNOWING THE REAL THING

One summer a friend of mine gave me some fresh garden green beans. I was glad to get them, as my plants had not started producing yet. I cooked them in my pressure cooker, and they tasted so good – as the first fresh green beans of summer always do.

The day after I cooked them, my son Jonathan came to do some electrical work for me. His three-year-old daughter came with him. For supper that night, we all enjoyed reheated green beans. However, Jonathan remarked, "These aren't Blue Lakes, are they." I admitted that they were not. (Blue Lake green beans are the variety I prefer to plant for canning – and eating – purposes.)

Please don't get me wrong – Jonathan enjoyed the green beans, having more than two servings. He just knew they were not Blue Lakes. He developed his preference through years of helping snap and can green beans.

The years we lived on a small city lot with no place for a garden took its toll on my children. They began to beg me to can green beans again, as they much preferred the home-canned variety over store-bought ones. At the time, I checked out the local farmer's market and became a regular customer. To show how much they wanted home canned beans, my children would help snap them with little to no complaining.

The parallel I want to draw here is this – we should know God's Word and hold to it above any other source of reference. While there are many good resources for us as Christians, the Bible should be our mainstay and the standard by which we measure anything else.

Jonathan knew the green beans he was eating were not Blue Lakes because he was very familiar with Blue Lakes. We should be able to tell when things are not Scriptural because we are very familiar with Scripture. Other people's writings and insights (including mine) need to take a lesser place to what the Word of God has to say to our lives. The Lord can (and does) use the influence of others to help us along the way. However, we should never substitute what people have to say for what God has to say.

> "Be diligent to present yourself approved to God as a workman who does not need to be ashamed, accurately handling the word of truth" (2 Timothy 2:15 NASB).

Day 3

PATTERNS

I have the ability to look at fabric and look at a pattern and picture the finished product in my mind. Sometimes it works beautifully; however, there are times, well, let's just venture to say that the completed project isn't exactly what I had pictured.

Sometimes the fabric I had chosen many not have been correct for the pattern style. Sometimes the pattern is fine for the slender models in the pattern pictures but for those of us with more well-padded figures the outcome turns out to be disastrous. For example, I had purchased a beautiful, shimmery piece of fabric. Woven from maroon and white threads, it ended up being a dark rose color. I found a pattern that looked like it would work well with the fabric and decided on a collar made with an embroidered white fabric. When I finished the dress, I was very pleased with how it looked. Then I put it on. My husband, Bob, ever tactful, said, "I think that dress makes you look a little–mmm–thick."

I decided to send the dress to my sister Terri. Although built a little differently than I am, we wear the same size. I thought that maybe it would work for her. However, her sons weren't as kind as Bob. "Mom, that dress makes you look FAT!" She was as devastated as I was because she loved the dress, too. We discussed all kinds of ways to alter it but couldn't come up with a workable solution.

Terri gave the dress to Cindy, who is the next in line of my three sisters. I never saw Cindy in it, but Terri said it looked nice on her. I never found out if Cindy wore the dress or not. Maybe she didn't want to take a chance on looking thick!

There are times that we decide that we would like to do a certain ministry. We think, "Boy, that would look good on me!" Sometimes God slams the door in our face. At other times, we jump in with both feet only to realize that we should never have gotten involved in that area in the first place; it wasn't really where we needed to be plugged in. We forget to ask the Father to show us clearly if that was what He had in mind for us to do. Then there are times we start something because we think there is no one else to do it. Soon we are up to our necks and want out, realizing that if God needed that particular job done, He would have provided someone who was gifted in that area.

On the positive side, there are times when the pattern and the fabric are perfect for each other, and the fit is just right. It is then that we feel like we are in the right place at the right time doing the right thing for God's honor and glory. And there is nowhere we would rather be!

> "Do not conform to the pattern of this world, but be transformed by the renewing of your mind. Then you will be able to test and approve what God's will is – his good, pleasing and perfect will" (Romans 12:2 NIV).

Day 4

DISCIPLINE FROM THE FATHER

When my son Jonathan was little, I often heard him carrying on conversations with himself. If I asked him to whom he was talking, he would reply, "Joey". Joey was one of those imaginary friends that some children have during childhood. He hung around with our family quite often. When asked where Joey lived, Jonathan answered, "In my mouth."

I don't think I will ever forget the day that I was preparing to punish Jonathan for talking back to me. He looked at me with his eyes as big as saucers. "Mom," he declared, "that wasn't me talking, it was Joey!" If Jonathan's mouth got him into trouble, it became Joey that got the blame. Jonathan seemed totally convinced that he should not get punished for things that Joey said.

How many times in our own lives do we refuse to accept the responsibility for our actions? We try to find a cause for our mistakes - somewhere else to place the blame. When directly confronted, we make excuses that we see as valid reasons for our actions. Being disciplined for our mistakes is not a pleasant thought, so we try to wiggle out of our punishment. We convince ourselves that we are not really at fault, so why should we be punished?

As parents, my husband and I had to deal with Jonathan's inappropriate behavior even when he blamed it on Joey. Jonathan is our child, and it was our job to make sure he understood that he had to take the responsibility for his own misdeeds. Our Heavenly Father God can see through all our excuses, and He allows us to suffer the consequences of our actions. Because we are His children, He disciplines us for not only our own good but also for the good of those around us. I am thankful that He cares enough to keep us on the right path!

"My son, do not despise the Lord's discipline, and do not resent his rebuke, because the Lord disciplines those he loves, as a father the son he delights in" (Proverbs 3:11-12 NIV).

Day 5

IT JUST BUGGED ME

I will remember as long as I live one of the times I spent several days with my cousin, who was the same age as me. Our mothers were first cousins, so that made us second cousins. My great-aunts Myrtle and Fay, who were sisters, lived with my cousin's family; Aunt Fay was her grandmother. Aunt Myrtle was my step-grandmother, having married my grandfather a few years after his wife (a sister to Myrtle and Fay), passed away. Aunt Myrtle did a lot of the cooking for the household.

My family lived in a regular neighborhood, but my cousin lived in a much more well-to-do area. Meals at her house included foods that my parents could not afford. Aunt Myrtle was an excellent cook, but there was one meal she prepared that will live forever in my memory.

My cousin and I were playing during the afternoon, and we often passed through the kitchen on our way to or from the screened in porch. On one of those trips, I noticed a pot sitting on the back burner of the stove. I was not tall enough to see into the pot, but I did notice what looked to be huge insect legs sticking out of the top of it. I kept trying to figure out what was in the pot but was unable to do so.

If there was ever a day I dreaded dinnertime, that was the day. I just knew we were going to be expected to eat giant bugs. I worried myself almost sick, especially when I would see those "legs" sticking out of the pot. My parents had always taught me that I was to eat whatever someone put on my plate. They had instilled in me that it was very rude to refuse food unless I had a legitimate reason (such as allergy) to do so.

At dinnertime, I did not feel very well and went to the table reluctantly. Much to my surprise, there were no huge insects on the table; not even anything that resembled a bug made an appearance. I was able to relax and enjoy my meal.

Upon my return home, I told my mother what had happened. She asked me what we had eaten for dinner that night. I don't remember now what we had except for one item. Beets. And I like beets. When she heard about the beets, Mom burst out laughing. She explained to me that when you cook fresh beets, you cut the leaves off the top but the stems need to remain on the beets. If you slice off the stems, the beets "bleed" all their color and flavor into the cooking water. I had never known that because our family ate canned beets. It was the beet stems sticking out of the top of the pot that had caused my afternoon of anguish.

Has there ever been something in your life that has you worried sick? Something that fills your soul with dread even though you know the Lord says not to worry? Now think to the time after it was over. Relief fills you. Your heart finally stops pounding, and your mouth has lost its dryness. You can let yourself go and relax. The issue often turns out to be anti-climactic compared to the anxiety you built up beforehand.

God's Word tells us not to live in fear and dread. We choose to do so anyway, but I have never figured out why. God never leaves us and never forsakes us. However, we take our eyes off Him like Peter did when he stepped out of the boat and began to sink–that is when the uneasiness steps in. Once it gets a foot in the door, it begins to grow and settle in for a long stay. And instead of taking a firm stand against it, we let it become a hindrance to our trust in God.

All I would have had to do to ease my fear of dinner that night was to ask Aunt Myrtle what was in the pot. She would have informed me of the contents, and I could have had a carefree afternoon. I chose to live in dread instead of finding out the answer. After all, what if she had told me it was some kind of insect?!

When the unknown has us in a tizzy, we need to turn to the Source of comfort and reassurance. God has given us so much and blessed us in so many ways. Our determination to trust in Him and let His guidance lead us through unsettled times will overcome the dread of what we cannot see.

"From my distress I called upon the LORD;
The LORD answered me and set me in a large place.
The LORD is for me; I will not fear;
What can man do to me?" (Psalm 118:5-6 NASB)

"Be anxious for nothing, but in everything by prayer and supplication with thanksgiving let your requests be made known to God. And the peace of God, which surpasses all comprehension, will guard your hearts and your minds in Christ Jesus" (Philippians 4:6-7 NASB).

Day 6

I GOT THE PICTURE

Have you ever been to a Revival meeting when they had a fill-a-pew night? The Revival that sticks out in my mind the most happened when I was about five years old. One of the nights was set aside for having children fill a pew; there were two prizes for the two top "contestants". The prizes were pictures of Jesus – if I remember correctly, one of them was a picture of Jesus blessing the children. The other one was a picture that is still familiar today – Jesus standing among sheep and holding a lamb. It was the top prize; it was the one I wanted. And I wanted it very badly.

Now, to put this story in perspective, you have to understand that I have battled shyness all of my life. Up until this point, my mom could hardly even get me to answer the telephone, let alone call someone on it. My sister Terri, who was the second child in our family (I am the oldest of six), has never had a shy bone in her body. But there have been many times that my shy nature has overcome a particular desire in my life. However, I wanted that picture so badly that I had my mom give me names and telephone numbers of people I could call to come to Revival services for that night. Terri remembers helping me, but all I remember is the panic I felt as I dialed the numbers and waited for the people I was calling to answer their telephones.

Mom had told me that if I wanted the picture, I had to call people myself. She was not going to do it for me. Once I told them who I was and what I wanted, I felt a vast relief. Some of the people I called were ones that I did not know personally, but they knew my parents. Others were relatives that realized how hard it was for me to call them because they knew how backward I was when it came to talking to other people.

Revival services that night were very crowded. Of course, I was not the only child that wanted one of those pictures. As a matter of fact, there were those in the congregation that thought they knew which two children would win the prizes. They were both older than I was and were far more outgoing. No one ever considered me to be in the running to be one of the winners. These two girls had already picked out which of the pictures they wanted. All they had to do was wait to be announced as the winners to take home their prizes. Imagine their surprise when more people stood up for me than for anyone else. The girl that was "supposed" to get the picture of Jesus and the sheep was very upset. She did not want the other picture. They tried to talk me into taking it, but I was adamant about which picture I wanted. It was the one that I had worked for, and I was not going to settle for the other one. It was finally decided to get another picture of Jesus and the sheep for her, and to give the picture of Jesus and the children to the third place winner.

The whole point of my telling this story is simply this: Never underestimate the underdog. All too often, we fail to realize how much some people have to offer because we don't know the determination that lies below their visible surface. Instead of drawing out their good qualities, we tend to push them aside as "non-contestants." We are quick to judge someone that is quiet and reserved as "stuck-up," as well as seeing people that are more loud and boisterous as non-serious and frivolous. We deny ourselves the wisdom and loyalty these people have to offer because they are not like us – or maybe they are more like us than we would like to think!

As fellow-laborers in God's kingdom, let's all make a point of looking for the hidden qualities that others have to offer. We never know what treasures we can find buried below their surface.

> "Let your speech always be with grace, as though seasoned with salt, so that you will know how you should respond to each person" (Colossians 4:6 NASB).

"…speaking the truth in love, we are to grow up in all aspects into Him who is the head, even Christ, from whom the whole body, being fitted and held together by that what every joint supplies, according to the proper working of each individual part, causes the growth of the body for the building up of itself in love" (Ephesians 4:15-16 NASB).

Day 7

OPEN THE DOOR AND LET ME IN

My cat Tennyson (who has now departed this life) enjoyed being with me. He would follow me around the house and if I went into a room and closed the door he would sit on the other side and cry to get in. When I holed up in my sewing room I often heard him meowing loudly – he wanted to be where I was. Tennyson often came and sat on my lap when I worked at the computer. There were times he stepped on the keyboard and messed up what I was doing. He wanted my attention and was not satisfied until he obtained it – all of it. He was not content with me being distracted by something else.

At some point in time, there must have been a deep-pile carpet in my house because the bottoms of the doors were cut off. (This happened before we moved here.) The carpet had been removed, leaving a large gap between the doors and the floor. When I refused to let Tennyson into the room with me, ignoring his loud howling and door banging, he would lie down in front of the closed door. However, since he wanted me to know that he was still there, he would stick one paw under the door as a reminder that I was neglecting him. And that paw usually remained there until I opened the door.

Tennyson could not turn a doorknob and open a door. I had to do it for him; if I did not choose to do so, he could not come to where I was. So many areas of our lives have closed doors. We are either afraid or unwilling to open those doors to the Lord's scrutiny. Even though He knows what lies behind them, He will not force His way in. We are required to open the doors.

Jesus tells us in Revelation 3:20-21: "Behold, I stand at the door and knock; if anyone hears My voice and opens the door, I will come in to him and will dine with him, and he with Me. He who overcomes, I will grant to him to sit down with Me on My throne, as I also overcame and sat down with My Father on His throne" (NASB). There were no closed doors between Jesus and His Father. We see an example of this in the Garden of Gethsemane when Jesus poured out His heart to God. He opened every door to every emotion he was feeling. He set an example for us, showing us that even though we open the doors, we may still have to endure trials. But we will overcome in the end, which is our ultimate goal.

Until we are willing to open those doors we keep closed to the Lord, He will gently remind us of His presence outside of them. He wants to be with us in everything; however, He will not enter forcefully. We are required to turn the knob to open each and every door that we have shut. Since we know He always has our best interests at heart, we can respond to Jesus and say, "I hear Your knock, and I'm opening the door!"

> "For everyone who asks receives; the one who seeks finds; and to the one who knocks, the door will be opened" (Luke 11:10 NIV).

Day 8

SHOE SHOPPING

Even though I have been aware of Him all my life, I still have to marvel at the way God works. His care for us is so very infinite and precious! It is hard to grasp just how much His love fills every nook and cranny of our lives.

Our closest neighbors were in their mid-seventies at the time. Because we live in a rural area, it is not uncommon for one of us to call the other if we need to go to town. Sometimes I will call to see if Anita wants to ride with me because we enjoy each other's company. Several years ago I had errands to run on the east side of Indianapolis, and I stopped by and picked her up on the way.

The last stop I had to make was at one of those stores that sells a little bit of everything. As we walked into the store, we were handed a sale flyer that had weekend specials, one of which was if you bought one pair of shoes you could get another pair for a penny. Anita told me she wanted to look at their shoes; I presumed she had seen the special. I showed her the location of the shoe department and then went to get my groceries.

Just as I was finishing my shopping, I spotted Anita, who had already been through the checkout. She was very excited because the store clerk informed her about the second pair of shoes when she purchased the pair in her cart. The clerk gave her a gift card for a second pair, and she wondered if she had enough time to run back and find one. We arranged a meeting place, and she hurried off to get her shoes.

Anita is very considerate of someone else's time, so she decided to get her shoes quickly without trying them on. She had purchased black athletic-style shoes and decided to get some white ones just like them, but unfortunately, they did not have any in her size. She decided to get another pair of black ones with Velcro closures instead of lace-ups, found a box labeled with her size, snatched them up, and went back through the checkout.

I thought nothing more about the shoe incident until a few days later when speaking to her by telephone. "Did I tell you about my second pair of shoes?" she asked. "When I got them home, the size printed on the box was different from the size in the shoes!" Upon further inspection, she discovered that she had picked up shoes from the men's department. So not only did she have shoes that were the wrong size, they were not even women's shoes.

Anita's husband Gerald sat watching her dilemma. "Let me see those," he declared, "maybe they will fit me." And sure enough, when he tried them on, they fit him perfectly! They were comfortable, and he liked the Velcro closures. An added benefit was that he did not have to go shopping to get shoes that fit him well.

Now, some people would say the whole thing was a coincidence. I choose to believe it was a loving Father taking care of His children utilizing one of His mysterious ways. His love is all around us; we just need to choose to see it.

> "Oh, the depth of the riches both of the wisdom and knowledge of God! How unsearchable are His judgments and unfathomable His ways!" (Romans 11:33 NASB).

> "How great is Your goodness,
> Which You have stored up for those who fear You,
> Which You have wrought for those who take refuge in You,
> Before the sons of men!" (Psalm 31:19 NASB).

Day 9

THAT'S MINE!

Have you ever heard two children fighting over something? Neither one wants to relinquish their claim because they would have to give up ownership to the contested object. "That's mine!" one of them will say. "No, it is not! You can't have it! It's mine!" And back and forth the argument goes. It can get even worse if still another child joins the argument, putting in a claim as well. Pretty soon the air is filled with angry voices and possibly even the sound of someone deciding to take physical action to establish ownership. The other possible scenario is for one of the children to give up possession, even though they are quite sure that they have a right to claim the object. They would rather have peace than to insist on their ownership.

There is also the flip side of the coin. When there is something to be done that no one wants to do, then you hear: "It is not my turn." "Make someone else do it! I did it last time." Or maybe the problem lies with a misplaced possession belonging to another person. "I didn't take it. Don't blame me!" "Maybe he took it, but I didn't!" "Look in her room and I'll bet you will find it!" All these statements are common replies to that scenario.

And then there are the times that you find something your children did not want you to find. "That is certainly not mine!" "I can't believe you thought I would have something like that!" "You know that you have told us not to bring those in the house. Do you really think that I didn't pay attention to what you said?"

We can be quick to claim that which would benefit us. We also can be quick to deny something that would cause us embarrassment or make us accept the blame for something that is our fault.

Now let's think back over the years to an object that no one wants but everyone deserves. A wooden cross that represents all our sins right down to the "little" white lies and "secret" ugly thoughts. As we look at the cross, we know it is ours to carry. Our guilt is undeniable. Even though we want to shout "It is not mine!" we cannot do so because it is ours. But just as we get ready to pick it up, we hear someone calling, "That is mine! I'll take it." Relief fills us as we realize that we don't have to claim the cross. Jesus claimed it for us. It was not His to take, nor was it beneficial for Him. However, unlike children who will not give up their claim to something that they consider rightfully theirs, we are more than happy to relinquish the ownership that we could establish to the cross.

Jesus did not say, "It's not my turn" or "Make someone else do it!" He refused to place the responsibility where it actually belonged when it would have been truthful for Him to state: "I didn't do it. Don't blame me." Instead, He accepted the cross, along with our sin and our shame, so that we could have life with Him. It was His act of unselfishly taking what did not belong to Him that bought us a pardon for our present and a hope for our future.

> "Make your own attitude that of Christ Jesus,
> who, existing in the form of God,
> did not consider equality with God
> as something to be used for His own advantage.
> Instead He emptied Himself
> by assuming the form of a slave,
> taking on the likeness of men.
> And when He had come as a man
> in His external form,
> He humbled Himself by becoming obedient
> to the point of death—
> even to death on a cross" (Philippians 2:5-8 HCSB).

> "For the wages of sin is death, but the gift of God is eternal life in Christ Jesus our Lord" (Romans 6:23 NIV).

Day 10

WINDING BOBBINS

I enjoy the feature of my sewing machine that allows me to change the bobbin without disturbing a work in progress. When I get ready to do more than one embroidery project, I wind several bobbins in preparation. I know when a bobbin is getting very low because my machine beeps so that I will realize that it is time to put in a full one. The same thing happens whether I am using the embroidery machine unit or just doing regular sewing. When prepared with a wound bobbin, I can just pop it in and keep right on going. I can't count the number of times I have thanked the Lord for this feature. It has saved me lots of headaches! If I run out of filled bobbins and need one, all I have to do is put an empty bobbin on the bobbin winder and use the auxiliary thread path to wind it. I still have no need to take my project out of the machine. As long as there is a bobbin on the bobbin winder, the machine will not sew.

I thought about how this could relate to prayer in our lives. As we get ready for each new day, we can begin it with prayer. I prepared for my sewing jobs by winding several bobbins ahead of time. In the same way, talking to the Father is the best way to prepare for what we will face– good, bad, or somewhere in between. There will be times that I will have to stop and take time out to change the bobbin or maybe even wind some more. And in our daily lives we still need to stop and take time out to pray. Sometimes we need to pray as we keep on working at what we are doing. Even though our prayers may not be quite as focused during that time, God still hears them and knows our hearts.

However, this type of praying is in addition to, not a substitution for, a time set aside for communication with the Lord.

On occasion, I have kept on sewing even when my machine beeps and tells me I am low on bobbin thread. I'll have just a few more inches to go and hope that I can make it to the end of my seam. Sometimes I can, but many times I will keep on sewing and realize that I ran out of bobbin thread several stitches back. That makes me think of times when we keep on going and don't make an effort to pray. Just like changing my bobbin would have saved re-doing part of a seam, taking the time to pray keeps us from forging ahead on our own when we need God's direction.

> "The Lord has heard my supplication,
> The Lord receives my prayer" (Psalm 6:9 NASB).

Day 11

RAISIN BREAD

One afternoon I asked my son Adam to make some bread in my bread machine. I had a particular recipe that I wanted him to use: Nutty Cinnamon Raisin Bread. It is very tasty and loaded with raisins and pecans. One feature found on many bread machines, including ours, is a timer that lets you know when it has five minutes or so left in the second kneading cycle. It beeps about ten times so that you can add raisins, nuts, or other ingredients that need to be mixed in but not pulverized. They get spread throughout the dough but keep their shapes and flavors.

As Christians in a sinful world, we need to have a distinct shape and flavor. Although we are mingled in with everyone else, others should be able to tell a difference in our speech and our actions. When we compromise our faith to be more like the world, we become like raisins added at the beginning of the bread cycle. They are kneaded so much by the paddle that they come apart and are blended in with the dough. They cannot be separated from the dough because they have become a part of it.

When Adam's bread was finished baking, cooled, and then sliced, I could see that the raisins and pecans were spread nicely throughout it, giving flavor to the whole loaf. If they had been in big clumps, the bread would not have been nearly as good. We need to make sure that we are spreading Christ's love to all those around us and not just those who are fellow-believers. Often, all it involves is just living Christ in front of people. They can tell the difference in us without our having to say a word. And when we do witness to them with our words it makes more of an impact because they have seen that our lives reflect what we are telling them about.

"Make every effort to live in peace with everyone and to be holy; without holiness no one will see the Lord" (Hebrews 12:14 NIV).

"And we all, who with unveiled faces contemplate the Lord's glory, are being transformed into his image with ever-increasing glory, which comes from the Lord, who is the Spirit" (2 Corinthians 3:18 NIV).

Day 12

CATCHING FLIES

Several years ago we had a Siamese cat named Proginoskes ("Progo" for short). One of his favorite pastimes was to catch flies. He would sit in the window and smack them with his front paws. It was funny to watch him eyeball a fly and then SMACK! The fly would fall to the windowsill dead. There came a day that it wasn't quite so funny. Unknowingly, Progo smacked a honeybee instead of a fly. When I saw his swollen paw, I looked at the windowsill; sure enough, a dead bee was lying there. Progo's foot got larger and larger as the day went on. I called the vet at home, as it happened to be a Sunday afternoon. He told me to give Progo a liquid allergy medication. The medicine eased Progo's pain, and he slept the rest of the day.

On Monday, poor Progo's paw was over twice its normal size, but he was feeling much better. He just had a huge front leg. The next thing I knew, there he was in the window, using that giant paw to smack a fly. He seemed quite pleased with the process; the size of that paw made it harder for the fly to get away!

There are many times in our lives that we have to deal with painful circumstances. Because they hurt so much, we feel that that portion of our life swells out of proportion to the rest of it. Our heavenly Father gives us the power we need to deal with these circumstances and go on. But we have to accept that power before it will be of use to us. I had the medication Progo needed to take to help with his bee sting. However, it did him no good until he swallowed it.

After much of the actual pain had gone away, Progo made use of his unfortunate circumstance. We can do the same in our lives even if it means nothing more than reaching out to others who may be experiencing their own set of problems. Seeing people use God's help to work through their problems gives hope to those around them. We all need to lean on the Lord. Since He lives in our hearts, we can hold each other up as we lean on Him Who Keeps Us from Falling.

> "Now to him who is able to keep you from stumbling, and to make you stand in the presence of His glory blameless with great joy, to the only God our Savior, through Jesus Christ our Lord, be glory, majesty, dominion and authority, before all time and now and forever. Amen" (Jude 24-25 NASB).

Day 13

ASPARAGUS, ANYONE?

I used to detest asparagus. My mother would probably tell you that seeing me eating asparagus willingly is a minor miracle.

Come spring, my dad would not only cut the asparagus plants in our yard, but he also knew where to find them growing along the roadside. So we usually had plenty of asparagus. I absolutely detested it. However, my parents were old-fashioned eat-what-is-on-the-table kind of people. There was no getting out of putting that nasty stuff into my mouth. If I didn't eat it for supper, I got it cold for breakfast the next morning. The only saving grace was that they allowed to smother it with salad dressing. I learned that with salad dressing on my asparagus, I would just have to swallow it and didn't have to chew. The sooner it got out of my mouth, the better I liked it.

Asparagus was not the only thing that my parents made me eat; it is just the thing that really stands out in my mind. Thank goodness they did not make me eat mushrooms, as I still don't like the thought of eating fungus. After years of eating things I did not like, I finally developed a taste for quite a few of them. And my old enemy asparagus became something that I now enjoy.

My children might tell you that their mother's upbringing was a disadvantage to them because I made them eat things that they did not like. I used to make them eat lima beans according to how old they were – one bean for each year. They were not allowed to go hunt through the cabinet or refrigerator for something they liked; they either ate what I put on the table or waited until the next meal. If they did not eat their meal, there was no snack in between meals. I was not quite the stickler that my parents were – each of them had strong dislikes to certain foods that they were not made to eat. Thankfully, my children all eat quite an assortment of vegetables, although there were times when I wondered if they ever would.

The Word of God is full of "vegetables"– things that are good for us even if we don't like them. We often want to leave out the parts that help us grow strong and healthy in our walk with Christ. If we had our way, we would choose the love of God and forget the wrath of God. We would skip the parts that make us uncomfortable because it can hurt to grow. We are so glad to enjoy God's forgiveness, but we find it hard to swallow the part that tells us that we must forgive others and ask their forgiveness when we are in the wrong. We want to cover up the sections that tell us about suffering being an integral part of the Christian life and smother them in feel-good theology. We feel so blessed to accept God's grace, yet it pains us to extend grace to fellow believers. And how about giving Jesus the Lordship of our lives? So many times we tell Him, "Please, I'd rather do it myself!" instead of letting Him have control.

We all have our "spiritual asparagus" – things that we find hard to swallow. Thankfully, God loves us enough to make sure our plates contain those things that are good for us, even when we rebel against consuming them.

> "Anyone who lives on milk, being still an infant, is not acquainted with the teaching about righteousness. But solid food is for the mature, who by constant use have trained themselves to distinguish good from evil" (Hebrews 5:13-14 NIV).

Day 14

FRUSTRATION OR BLESSING?

We took a trip to North Carolina one year; it rained every day that we were there. Besides that, the temperatures were about 30 degrees lower than normal for that time of year. I had read a "local attractions" book that I found in our hotel room and picked out some things I wanted to see. They had an arboretum and some gardens that I especially wanted to visit. Needless to say, we did not get a chance to go there due to the rain. But what was an aggravation to us was a blessing to that area. They had been short on rainfall and desperately needed these wet days. While I was wishing it would stop raining, people there were praying for it to keep on coming down.

Sometimes the things in our lives that are an aggravation to us may be a blessing to someone else. A red light that slows us down may let someone else proceed on an urgent journey. The busy signal we hear on the other end of the line could tell us that the party we dialed received a long-awaited important call. Just like the rain that was a frustration for me was "showers of blessing" to the people in North Carolina that year. When you feel frustrated about the way things are going, ask yourself if the things that have blessed you have been a frustration to someone else. Makes you think twice, doesn't it?

"Be glad in the Lord, you righteous ones,
And give thanks to His holy name" (Psalm 97:12 NASB).

Day 15

PIGEON, ANYONE?

Our family lived on a busy street corner for most of the years my children were in school. We had an older home with a large front porch, and I often enjoyed warm, sunny days while sitting on the porch swing watching the world going by. However, one particular spring my pastime became filled with frustration due to some pigeons that decided the ledges around our front porch pillars would be a good place for nesting.

No matter how many times we removed the nests, the pigeons kept coming back. Someone suggested that mothballs might discourage them. The pigeons didn't care. They just pushed the mothballs off the ledges and went right on building their nests. Time and again we took a hose and sprayed the bits of grass and twigs off the columns. The pigeons decided to lay their eggs anyway. It became a real battle.

Finally, we were able to stop the nest building, at least for a while. Then came the day that a small pigeon that made its way to our porch. It looked rather ill, but it had enough strength to flop away from me every time I tried to catch it. Since I did not want a sick bird on my porch, I decided to call for professional help.

The man who came to my house was no spring chicken; as a matter of fact, he was well on the other end of the spectrum. When I explained my problem, he proceeded to try to catch the pigeon with his bare hands. The pigeon, of course, was having NOTHING to do with that idea!

I wondered why the man did not use a net, but he informed me that he did not bring one with him. I must admit that I was quite surprised – he knew he was coming after a bird, so why would he not have a net? The next thing I knew, the bird managed to flutter its way up to the ledge on a corner column of the porch. Before I realized what was happening, the rather elderly man climbed onto the side wall of the porch and was standing on the ledge trying to catch the pigeon. I was feeling rather panicked because there was quite a drop to the bushes below, and I feared he would lose his balance and fall off the porch.

The pigeon, tired of being chased, fluttered completely off the porch and into the side yard of our home. A state highway ran alongside this particular stretch of our property. It was at this point that the man who had come to help me with the pigeon asked if I had some bread. After I had inquired the purpose, he informed me he was going to try to lure the bird with the crumbs. I had some stale crackers that I "donated" to his "cause".

The man began walking toward the bird and tossing crumbs at it. "Here, bird! Here, bird!" he began to call in a very nasally voice. I could not take it anymore. I had to go in the house. The laughter bubble that was building inside was going to burst at any moment. Thankfully it waited until I closed the door. I laughed so hard that my sides hurt, and tears were rolling down my cheeks.

When I was finally able to control myself, I watched out the window. The man followed the bird around to the other side of the house, all the time calling "Here, bird! Here, bird." He was taking out crackers, crumbling them, and tossing the crumbs as he went. Just as he would get close to the pigeon, it would flutter away. It finally managed to flap its way over the privacy fence that separated the front yard from the back.

At that point, I went back out on the porch. The "professional" came back around the house, wiping his brow as he walked. That is when he informed me that he could not catch the bird. "Ma'am," he proclaimed, "this here is a love bird. It knows you have a loving home, and it has decided to live here with you. There is nothing wrong with it; it is just young and still learning

31

to fly. You should feel honored that it chose your home." With that said, he got into his truck and drove away, leaving me standing there with my mouth hanging open in disbelief.

I managed to propel myself to the front door and go inside. It took a few moments for the shock to wear off and then the hilarity of the situation hit me all over again. In modern terminology, I was ROTFL (for those who are less savvy it means "rolling on the floor laughing").

While re-living this story in my mind, I thought of an application for it.

The man came to catch a bird but brought no net – in other words, he came into a situation without the right equipment, leaving him unable to do the job he came to perform. We as Christians have a wonderful tool - the word of God. How often do we go into situations and forget to carry the very thing that equips us to be equal to the task at hand?

That doesn't necessarily mean we should take a Bible everywhere we go, as we are supposed to have God's Word in our hearts. The Holy Spirit brings to mind those things we have learned when we ask for wisdom in any situation we may face. Our job is to remember to use the tools we possess and to keep prepared by staying in God's Word.

The second lesson from my story is this: Many times we realize that there are things in our lives we need to discard. However, there are those people that would have us believe it is okay to keep them. We know we should dispose of them, yet we have become too comfortable with having them with us. They are things like envy, greed, lust, procrastination, foul language, idolatry (things that take first place in our lives instead of God), and questionable entertainment. The list could go on and on. We want to be like those around us, so we are none too eager to remove them. But just like the bird did NOT belong on my front porch despite what the kind-hearted man declared, so these things do not belong in the life of one of God's children.

Tying the two lessons together, we should realize that if God's Word is entrenched in our hearts, we will more readily discern the things that don't belong there. Our love of God will help us to get rid of them, knowing that

He always has our best interests at heart and wants us to live free of the encumbrances of sin.

"Let no one deceive you with empty words, for because of these things the wrath of God comes upon the sons of disobedience. Therefore do not be partakers with them; for you were formerly darkness, but now you are Light in the Lord; walk as children of Light (for the fruit of the Light consists in all goodness and righteousness and truth), trying to learn what is pleasing to the Lord" (Ephesians 5:6-10 NASB).

"So put out of your life every evil thing and every kind of wrong. Then in gentleness accept God's teaching that is planted in your hearts, which can save you. Do what God's teaching says; when you only listen and do nothing, you are fooling yourselves. Those who hear God's teaching and do nothing are like people who look at themselves in a mirror. They see their faces and then go away and quickly forget what they looked like. But the truly happy people are those who carefully study God's perfect law that makes people free, and they continue to study it. They do not forget what they heard, but they obey what God's teaching says. Those who do this will be made happy" (James 1:21-25 NCV).

Day 16

A PUDGY FOOTSTOOL

My Aunt Barbara and Uncle Herbert used to have a Pekingese dog named Pudgy. He was a cute little guy, with lots of long fur. He looked like a mobile rug, or possibly a short footstool. My sister Cindy must have opted for the footstool idea. She was a toddler at the time and decided that Pudgy was just the right height to make a good seat for her. She would back up to him and slowly start to sit down. Pudgy would move just enough to get out of Cindy's range, and she would land on her backside. Picking herself up off the ground, Cindy would look at Pudgy standing there so still, gauge the distance, and back up to him again. Pudgy waited until Cindy was in the process of sitting down and then he would move again, but not very far. This process had happened several times before someone intervened and either called the dog or retrieved Cindy. I only remember the determination of both Cindy and Pudgy. She was determined to sit on him, and he was equally determined that he was not a stool, and he was not going to stand still for that kind of abuse (pun intended).

Cindy's mistake was in choosing a shifting object instead of a solid surface on which to park her little derriere. There were plenty of places she could have sat that would not have moved; however, she chose what looked to be a comfy seat. Those of us who were watching were highly amused at the incident; it still sticks in my mind after all these years.

Life is full of things that look as if they might make a comfortable place to relax. Jobs, family, education, hobbies – the list could go on and on. Just when we think we can let go and be comfortable, the very things we rely on can shift. Jobs are lost or changed into something not so familiar. Family members can cause issues in so many ways: moving away, severing relationships for some reason or other, become ill, pass away, etc. Education is never an end in and of itself; there is always more to learn. Hobbies help us pass the time but are nothing to base our lives around.

Thankfully, there is one thing on which we can depend. The love of God never fails. God is always reliable and will not change when we decide to rest upon His grace and mercy. He will not move away from our dependence on Him. I find it wonderful to know that my life can have such a solid place to relax and know that I will be supported.

"For I, the Lord, do not change" (Malachi 3:6a NASB).

"Every good thing given and every perfect gift is from above, coming down from the Father of lights, with whom there is no variation or shifting shadow" (James 1:17 NASB).

Day 17

ELECTRIC BLANKET WOES

My husband Bob worked for many years as an electrician. A friend of ours asked him to check out her electric blanket. She is quite cold natured, and it wasn't getting her warm. The funny thing about it was that the blanket was getting warm on top, just not on the bottom. Bob tested it out electrically and everything seemed to be working fine. He was puzzled about the situation until he realized where the problem lay. Our friend had put a thermal blanket in between the electric blanket and the top sheet. It was doing a good job of keeping the warm coming out of the electric blanket from soaking down into the area below it. Once the thermal blanket was placed on top of the electric one, everything worked fine.

This scenario caused me to think about how that thermal blanket is like things we put in between ourselves and God. We fail to feel the full effects of the warmth of God's love and mercy because we have erected a barrier where there should not be one. Often, we picture God as too much like ourselves. We lose sight of His Divinity in the light of our humanity. When we struggle with a problem, we think maybe God is having a problem with us. This perceived problem creates an even thicker barrier in our minds between our heavenly Father and us.

God is so awesome and infinite that our minds cannot conceive the whole of Him. We try hard to categorize and describe Him; we want to understand Who He is and what He requires of us. However, we neglect to let Him be all He can be in our lives because we are too busy trying to figure Him out. It is when we let go of our own perceptions of Him, pulling out the barriers we have erected, that we experience the full warmth of God's presence in our lives.

"I know that you can do all things; no plan of yours can be thwarted. You asked, 'Who is this that obscures my counsel without knowledge?' Surely I spoke of things I did not understand, things too wonderful for me to know. You said, 'Listen now, and I will speak; I will question you and you shall answer me.' My ears had heard of you but now my eyes have seen you. Therefore I despise myself and repent in dust and ashes" (Job 42:2-6 NIV).

"Return to your rest, my soul, for the Lord has been good to you" (Psalm 116:7 HCSB).

Day 18

HOLD ON (WAIT)

Several years ago, my husband Bob and I were traveling back home to Indiana from Illinois. We were accompanied by our granddaughter who had just turned 4. There was a discussion going on as to whether or not we had turned the wrong way on I-64. We were headed east but were trying to figure out if we had missed our connection to the highway connecting I-64 to I-70. In the middle of our interchange, Maggie asked me if I would turn on the kids' songs because she wanted to listen to them. My answer to Maggie was, "Hold on a minute. You can listen to them in a little bit."

After my reply, Maggie was quiet for several minutes. Then in a matter-of-fact voice she stated, "Grammie, I don't think I like 'hold on'. I think it makes me a little bit aggravated." I thought Bob was going to burst from trying not to laugh out loud!

As I remembered this little incident, I began to wonder about how many times God hears the same thing from His children when He tells us to wait. We pray and expect God to answer immediately and in the way we desire Him to act. I think we can accept a "No" better than we deal with a "Hold on". When God closes doors we know that He has something else in mind for us, but the times He asks us to "wait" can be very frustrating for the impatient people we have become.

Although God may tell us to wait, it does not mean that He is unaware of our needs and desires. It does not mean that He is uncaring about our circumstances. We may not see His hand at work; however, that does not imply that He is somehow ignoring His children.

Waiting does not come easy even for those of us in the family of God. It is hard for us to learn to relax in the knowledge that God is in control, and He will make things happen in His time, in His way, and for our ultimate good.

> "Though youths grow weary and tired,
> And vigorous young men stumble badly,
> Yet those who wait for the Lord
> Will gain new strength;
> They will mount up with wings like eagles,
> They will run and not get tired.
> They will walk and not become weary" (Isaiah 41:30-31 NASB).

When we learn to wait on the Lord, He gives us a testimony:
> "I waited patiently for the Lord;
> And He inclined to me and heard my cry.
> He brought me up out of the pit of destruction, out of the miry clay
> And He set my feet upon a rock making my footsteps firm.
> He put a new song in my mouth, a song of praise to our God;
> Many will see and fear
> And will trust in the Lord" (Psalm 40:1-3 NASB).

Day 19

REFLECTING HIM

Our dog Nika was on a leash; she and I were walking beside the fence on the creek side of our property. The sun was shining brightly, and we were enjoying the beautiful weather. I noticed something several yards in front of us that was reflecting the sun; it was sending large beams of light back toward the sky. I thought it was probably a large piece of glass or metal – the man who owned the property before us had lots and lots and lots of old cars and parts stored all over it. When Nika and I came close to the place where the reflections had originated, I was surprised to see that there was no big piece of anything. There were only a few small black bits of some unknown substance that were lying there bouncing the sun's rays heavenward.

There are times in life that we can feel like a "nobody" – just some minor part of creation that is not useful for very much. We may not see ourselves as a part of the "great scheme of things"; we feel more like useless debris than a diamond in the rough. But we have a great God, who can use us no matter how we feel. If we are reflecting the love of His Son to others, we are doing immeasurably more than we realize. Sometimes it is those who feel the most insignificant that become major players in the kingdom of God.

If you are feeling more like rubbish than something useful, remember that the Father of Light is shining down upon you. Make up your mind to spread that light to all those around you and realize that in so doing, you become a brilliant reflection of the love of God. You may never know the effect you have on others until you reach Heaven, but you can rest assured that the "Son-beams" you reflect will leave a legacy far beyond your wildest imagination!

"For you were once darkness, but now you are light in the Lord. Live as children of light (for the fruit of the light consists in all goodness, righteousness and truth) and find out what pleases the Lord. ... But everything exposed by the light becomes visible – and everything that is illuminated becomes a light. This is why it is said: 'Wake up, sleeper, rise from the dead, and Christ will shine on you'" (Ephesians 5:8-10, 13-14 NIV).

Day 20

WHY THE CHICKEN CROSSED THE ROAD

My person opinion: because it had a death wish!

Some years ago I was taking my daughter to the dentist. We were running close on time, so I was hoping for no delays. Down the road from us there are curves that force you to slow down. I was preparing to accelerate after going through the curves when a chicken decided to cross the road. It took its own sweet time strutting to the other side. I was creeping along slowly, almost to a point of stopping, when the chicken stepped into the grass and off the road. I lifted my foot off the brake and was getting ready to press the accelerator when the chicken got a wild look in its eye. It turned around, making a mad dash for the side of the road from whence it had come in the first place.

I tried to stop, but the tell-tale "thump, thump" informed me that my efforts to avoid the chicken had failed. A glance in my rearview mirror revealed that cartoons are correct; feathers DO swirl around in a circle above a bird that has met an untimely end. My daughter and I burst into laughter, but not because the chicken was dead. The wild look in its eye as it made a mad dash for the other side of the road caused us to believe it might have had suicidal thoughts. The swirling feathers just added to our mirth. I asked my daughter if she thought I should stop and tell the people that I had hit their chicken. She stopped laughing long enough to reply, "Mom, they aren't going to think you're very sorry about it when you are laughing so hard!" We went on to the dentist. When we came back, the chicken was gone.

There is no way I could have known that the chicken was going to decide to return to its starting place. I was just happy that it had finally reached the other side of the road and was, or so I thought, where it wanted to be. But the pull of what it had left behind must have been strong enough to cause it to throw caution to the wind and make the mad dash that led to its demise. (Maybe since it was a red chicken it was attracted to my red minivan ...)

Too many Christians get caught in this same kind of setup. They start out with the goal of making it to "the other side" (Heaven) and are diligent at pressing on to the prize of their high calling. Then something triggers them to look back. Life on the other side attracts their attention once again. Unable to keep themselves focused on Christ, they make a mad dash for the wrong side of the road, unaware that Satan is ready to run them down as they go back into a life of sin. They may not suffer physical death, but their spirit becomes numb to the calling of the Most High God.

My heart aches for the poor souls who have left their faith to follow the world and its elusive happiness. My prayer is that they will be restored to their Savior, realizing that spiritual death is a far more serious problem than being unhappy in this life. Abiding joy has only one source – it comes from the Creator of All Things and being in tune with Him.

> "But I say, walk by the Spirit, and you will not carry out the desire of the flesh. For the flesh sets its desire against the Spirit, and the Spirit against the flesh; for these are in opposition to one another, so that you may not do the things that you please" (Galatians 5:16-17 NASB).

> "Brethren, even if anyone is caught in any trespass, you who are spiritual, restore such a one in a spirit of gentleness; each one looking to yourself, so that you too will not be tempted. Bear one another's burdens, and thereby fulfill the law of Christ" (Galatians 6:1-2 NASB).

Day 21

A GIFT OF LAUGHTER

I firmly believe that the Lord provides times of laughter during certain seasons of our lives. A good laugh has been proven to be beneficial to a person's health and who else but our Great Physician could have blessed us with such a fun way to reduce our tension levels?

Life does have its periods of stress. Not all of it is bad; however, change in itself can bring with it a great deal of pressure and anxiety. As things build up, God keeps providing lighter moments to brighten our days. Here is a prime example:

I had a veterinary appointment for two of our outside cats. Midnight and Roosevelt were siblings, coming from a line of stray cats that found their way to our home after we moved to the country. We liked having cats around because they kept the rodent population down; this was especially helpful during harvest time on a property surrounded by farm fields. The two cats were already spayed and neutered; their vet appointment was for their yearly checkup and shots.

After the cats had been weighed in, we were placed in what I like to think of as the "cat room". It had a large wallpaper border of cats sitting among flower pots. The border was about 12 inches tall and went all around the room— the top of it was even with the tops of the doors.

Midnight and Roosevelt had never lived inside. They were uncomfortable with being cooped up, and Midnight was especially skittish. During the appointment, she decided that she had endured enough humiliation after getting her temperature taken rectally. She glanced at the mini-blind covered window–the blind was open allowing her to see outside–and decided to make a jump to freedom. Thankfully, she was a petite six pounds because her head managed to poke between some of the slats and her front legs found their way between others. The metal blind was all splayed out from the unaccustomed weight of a little black cat struggling desperately to get out of what she perceived as danger. I managed to control my laughter even though I was quite amused at the sight.

One of my cat carriers was sitting on the metal examination table; the other one was on one of two chairs that were side-by-side against the wall. Roosevelt had been slinking around the room looking for a way to get out. As I was calming Midnight after her blind adventure, Roosevelt thought he found his way of escape. He leaped onto the empty chair, jumped on the cat carrier, and then catapulted himself towards the cats in the wallpaper border, crashing into the wall with a thud. I stood there in disbelief as he slid down the wall, landed on the floor, and walked nonchalantly away as if nothing out of the ordinary had happened. By this time, I would normally have been bent over double with screams of laughter but I remembered where I was and succeeded in stifling my mirth.

I had forgotten about the whole incident until my husband asked me if I had read the "Arlo and Janis" cartoon strip in that night's paper. He then proceeded to show it to me. When I saw the cartoon cat crashing into something, the whole scenario at the vet's office replayed in my head. Bob thought my outburst of laughter was a bit overdone for the humor in the cartoon, but he joined me in a fit of hilarity when I described my visit at the veterinarian.

God has infinite care for His children, and He knows when we need some amusement in our lives. Doses of merriment keep us going and help us regain perspective and focus. Thanks be to the Lord for His gift of laughter!

> "Behold, this is the joy of His way;
> And out of the dust others will spring.
> Lo, God will not reject a man of integrity,
> Nor will He support evildoers.

He will yet fill your mouth with laughter
And your lips with shouting" (Job 8:19-21 NASB).

"Many are saying, 'Who will show us any good?'
Lift up the light of Your countenance upon us, O Lord!
You have put gladness in my heart,
More than when their grain and new wine
abound" (Psalm 4:6-7 NASB).

"But let all who take refuge in You be glad,
Let them ever sing for joy;
And may You shelter them,
That those who love Your name may exult in You.
For it is You who blesses the righteous man, O Lord,
You surround him with favor as with a shield" (Psalm 5:11-12).

Day 22

BLESS THE DISHWASHERS

I spent an afternoon baking pies – I had three pumpkin pies in the oven, filling for a peach cobbler cooking on the stove, and a crust rolled out and in the pan for a pecan pie. I was just getting ready to make the filling for it when my then-teenage daughter Molly decided to come out of her hidey-hole and help me. Of course, she was not interested in working on the mound of dirty dishes that had built up. She wanted to make the pecan pie filling. So she took over the pie making, and I did the dishes. Since the pecan pie turned out well, Molly got the praise for pie baking. (She also made the crust for the peach cobbler.)

I have not related this to show that I was jealous of Molly for making the pie that won praise; after all, who taught her to cook?! But I do know who spent the majority of time in the kitchen – me. And I know who washed ALL the dishes: it was not Molly. I stood in front of the sink with my hands in the dishwater. I began to think of the many times we hear this prayer before meals: "Bless this food and the hands that prepared it." But how often do you hear: "Bless the hands that wash the dishes afterward"? I don't think I have ever heard that prayer. The dishwasher could be - and often is - the same person (or persons) that cooked the meal. However, there may be people involved in the cleanup process that did not contribute to the preparation.

We often forget to pray for the "dishwashers" in our local congregations as well. It is much easier to remember to pray for the "up front" people than it is to remember to pray for those who work behind the scenes. When praying for the minister, don't forget his wife and family. We should remember to pray for our teachers– they spend a lot of time in lesson preparation. And what about elders, deacons, custodians, office workers, those who prepare communion, and nursery workers? The list could go on and on. It takes many "behind the scenes" volunteers to keep things running smoothly. Even if we don't know specific names, God does.

Have you ever heard someone say, "You did a nice job on the dishes."? Not only should we pray for "dishwashers", we also need to encourage them. We can use anything from a thank you note to a simple comment. Hearing "Nice job!" or "Way to go!" creates a warm feeling of being appreciated. If we take the time to brighten someone else's day, maybe we will receive a blessing in kind when it is our turn to do the dishes.

"Therefore encourage one another and build each other up, just as in fact you are doing" (1 Thessalonians 5:11 NIV).

"To sum up, all of you be harmonious, sympathetic, brotherly, kindhearted, and humble in spirit; not returning evil for evil, or insult for insult, but giving a blessing instead; for you were called for the very purpose that you might inherit a blessing" (I Peter 3:8-9 NASB).

Day 23

FAMILIARITY

My husband, Bob, was helping me clean up after Sunday dinner. He turned on the garbage disposal to get rid of some potato peelings that were in the sink. When I walked into the kitchen, the disposal was making a horrible noise, and Bob was just standing there. I told him that it sounded like there was something in the disposal that shouldn't be; he said it was just potato peels and that it was okay. I have ground up several potato peels in that garbage disposal, and I could tell by the racket that there weren't JUST potato peels in it. I told him, rather loudly, I must admit, to "TURN IT OFF!" Sure enough, when I reached into the disposal, my green scratcher pad was all in shreds. Thank goodness it was nothing worse than a scratcher pad. (I have gotten dishcloths stuck in there, and they don't shred ... they just jam up the disposal, plus I have a spoon that was permanently disfigured by its garbage disposal incident.)

The point I want to make is this. Bob and I heard the same thing, but only one of us realized that something was not right. I am usually the one that runs the disposal, so I am familiar with the noises that it makes. Because it didn't sound like it should, I knew to check it out. The same thing can be said of our walk with the Lord. If we are aware of how the Holy Spirit works in our lives and are listening for His influence, we can tell when to stop and check things out. We know we should not ignore His voice and just keep on doing what we have been. The Lord helps us to recognize that there may be disaster ahead if we proceed without paying attention to what He has to say.

"But the Helper, the Holy Spirit, whom the Father will send in My name, He will teach you all things, and bring to your remembrance all that I said to you" (John 14:26 NASB).

Day 24

IT HAPPENED IN FOURTH GRADE

I had always loved school—and still did after that year was over—but one of the very worst school experiences that I ever had happened during fourth grade. There was a first-grade boy that lived in our neighborhood who hated school. He would do anything possible so he would not have to go. Unfortunately for me, his mother asked my mother if I would be responsible for seeing that he arrived safely at school in the mornings. Besides getting myself to school, I had to make sure that two of my sisters and this little boy, along with his older sister, walked the mile to school every day. And I had to be sure that we all arrived before the tardy bell rang.

One particular morning, we had stopped by for our neighbors and were headed to school. The little boy had been crying and saying he was sick, but since that was par for the course, we just ignored him. Then he WAS sick—all over the sidewalk. I threw my books down on a stone wall and took him back home. The rest of our crew went on ahead; I barely had time to grab my books and make it to school before the tardy bell. My teacher's rule was that our homework had to be turned in as soon as we came into the classroom. I pulled mine out of my book and placed it on the stack with everyone else's, managing to get into my seat just in the nick of time. Keep in mind, this was in the days before book bags were a popular item.

My teacher would grade our homework during the school day, and then she would read out our grades towards the end of the day. On this day, as she stood in front of the class preparing to report our scores, she gave us a lecture on irresponsibility. She held up a paper that had been in contact with bird droppings and proceeded to say how awful it was that someone would turn in that paper. I cringed, realizing what had happened. When I had thrown my books down on the retaining wall, my paper had managed to land in bird waste. The teacher then stuck that paper on the bottom of the stack and began to read out the grades, which were always in numerical order, highest down to lowest. As she got further down the list, and my name had not been called, I knew without a doubt that the paper on the bottom was mine. I always made excellent grades in math, and it was the math homework that she was handing out. Sure enough, the last grade that she read was a 100, and it was my paper. Everyone stared at me as I received my soiled homework. The teacher gave me a look that would kill. I could feel my face burning, and I wanted to sink into the floor. I was totally humiliated. For a child who was as shy as me, it was a totally devastating experience. Even though I knew that my paper had gotten messed up trying to help someone else, I also knew that my teacher never wanted to hear excuses for anything.

Have you ever done something to help someone else and ended up causing problems for yourself because of it? And no matter what excuse you come up with, it even sounds lame to your own ears, let alone the person who is hearing it. It has probably happened to all of us at some point or another. We feel unjustly accused, and sometimes we want to crawl into a hole and lick our wounds. However, the one who really counts knows our hearts, and He is the one we will give account to in the end. Life may not seem fair, but we must stop and realize that the sacrifices and suffering that we experience on earth will make Heaven just that much sweeter when we get there!

"God is not unjust; he will not forget your work and the love you have shown him as you have helped his people and continue to help them. We want each of you to show this same diligence to the very end, so that what you hope for may be fully realized. We do not want you to become lazy, but to imitate those who through faith and patience inherit what has been promised" (Hebrews 6:10-12 NIV).

Day 25

PENCIL STUBS

I like to keep pencils, pens, and markers in a cup. I managed to knock the cup over one day, and as I was picking them up, I noticed something. Most of the pencils were either short stubs with erasers that were almost complete or the pencils were about three-quarter length with no eraser. I don't remember seeing any of them where the lead use and the eraser use were equal.

A pencil lead is the "output" side. It is what makes a pencil useful. An eraser, on the other hand, is to get rid of errors. It depends on how many mistakes we make as to which will be used up first: the lead or the eraser.

If we compare life to a pencil, at the end of my life, I want to be like the pencil stub with much more eraser than lead. I know that I make many mistakes, but I would hope that the productive side of my life generates far more usage than the clean-up side. How sad it would be to think most of my life had been spent getting rid of goof-ups instead of working to build up the Kingdom of God.

How is your pencil doing? Let's all work to make sure we are using our lead much faster than our erasers!

"Good and upright is the Lord; therefore
he instructs sinners in his ways.
He guides the humble in what is right and teaches them his way.

All the ways of the Lord are loving and faithful toward
those who keep the demands of his covenant.
For the sake of your name, Lord, forgive
my iniquity, though it is great.
Who, then, are those who fear the Lord? He will
instruct them in the ways they should choose.
… Guard my life and rescue me; do not let me
be put to shame, for I take refuge in you.
May integrity and uprightness protect me, because my
hope, Lord, is in you" (Psalm 25:8-12, 20-21 NIV).

Day 26

STICKY SITUATION

I was in our utility room, struggling to place something on top of our upright freezer. In the process, I managed to knock a can of lemon-lime soda onto the floor. When it hit the concrete, it popped open and rolled toward the kitchen, spewing its sugary contents all over everything in its path. My cat Tennyson was standing beside my feet and managed to get a good soaking. He leapt straight up off the floor; his tail fluffed out like a round hairbrush. He ran towards the kitchen with the can coming right behind him. He jumped again and finally managed to escape the hissing soda fountain.

Now I had a huge mess to clean up. There were drops of sticky liquid all over the freezer, the washer, and the dryer; not to mention what was soaking into the basket of laundry I had just finished folding. Right back into the washer it went.

Tennyson was a much more difficult clean-up job than the clothes. If you have ever bathed a cat with sticky fur, then you have my sympathy. Tennyson did NOT like the shower that he had to endure. He meowed so loudly that anyone within earshot would have thought I was trying to drown him. My son's cat sat outside the bathroom door and added his "what's going on in there" cries to Tennyson's "HELP! Get me out of here!" howls. Tennyson's fur was quite thick, so it took two large towels to get him dry enough to finish the job with a blow dryer. Needless to say, he was less than impressed with the noise it made. I finally managed to get him dry enough to let him go and finish drying on his own.

Have you ever been somewhere at the wrong time and ended up in a sticky situation? Maybe it involved someone just letting off steam, but how you wished you could run away. The person who was upset spewed forth accusations and inferences toward somebody else, or possibly several people. You had never perceived that person or those people in that way. Then you wondered if you should view them differently, whether the information is true or not. The sticky residue was there to be cleaned up, and you had to do the cleaning, even though you were just an innocent bystander. And the clean-up was none too easy. You kept finding drops of doubt about the people who had been the subjects of the accusations.

And then there are times that we ourselves are the "spew-er". We think that it is our duty to inform people about how someone else has mistreated us, or how much we are unappreciated. When we try to make ourselves look better by making others look worse, we leave not only a bad impression of others but also of ourselves. If we aren't careful, maligning others becomes a part of our everyday lives, reducing our effectiveness in the kingdom of God. Then the cleanup becomes even harder.

Just remember this: when something sticky has a chance to dry, it can be even harder to clean up. So if you find yourself in a sticky situation, whether you are the recipient or the cause, get out your cleaning supplies!

> "My dear brothers and sisters, take note of this: Everyone should be slow to speak and slow to become angry, because human anger does not produce the righteousness that God desires" (James 1:19-20 NIV).

Day 27

CHASING A TAIL

We had a kitten named Pemberton, who loved to chase his tail. I have seen many cats go after their tails before, but Pemberton had more dedication than most. He resembled a white whirlwind as he spun around and around. (Some days I thought we could use him for a fan!) He would be going clockwise, stop for a second, and then suddenly start twirling around in a counter-clockwise direction. But no matter how fast he went, his tail eluded his grasp. As he began to tire and his rotation became slower and slower, his tail went slower as well. When he finally flopped down, he was able to catch it.

Watching Pemberton chase after something that has been his all along caused me to realize how often we as Christians do the same thing. We seek after peace and joy and meaning for our lives; however, God has given both already. But we run frantically in circles, chasing after that which seems to elude us no matter how many revolutions we make. It is only when we slow down and give up the chase that we come to understand that our efforts have been in vain. Not because we can never have peace and joy and meaning for our lives, but because we already have them.

Our Faithful God always keeps His promises; His Word is full of promises to give us the very things we are running after. And we need not search for what we already have. So let's stop chasing and start enjoying!

"Peace I leave with you; my peace I give you. I do not give to you as the world gives. Do not let your hearts be troubled and do not be afraid" (John 14:27 NIV).

"Yet he has not left himself without testimony: He has shown kindness by giving you rain from heaven and crops in their seasons; he provides you with plenty of food and fills your hearts with joy" (Acts 14:17 NIV).

"Now there are different gifts, but the same Spirit. There are ministries, but the same Lord. And there are different activities, but the same God activates each gift in each person. A demonstration of the Spirit is given to each person to produce what is beneficial" (1 Corinthians 12:4-7 HCSB).

Day 28

HOLDING ON TO JESUS

I have laughed and laughed about one of my granddaughter Vivian's adventures. (She was 26 months old at the time.) My son Jonathan posted a picture of Vivian on social media. She was standing facing a manger. She had on a lovely Christmas dress (which I recognized even from the backside); however, she was also wearing a sheep head. I could see other children behind the manger. Jonathan's caption went like this: "Security footage from the scene of the crime - it seems a little sheep stole baby Jesus from the Christmas Play this Sunday morning."

In a comment line, I questioned if the sheep should look familiar. Jonathan replied: "The sheep is convinced that the evidence is inconclusive, but there were several eyewitness accounts indicating that said sheep escaped quickly down the aisle with what could have been baby Jesus hidden in some swaddling clothes. A source close to the alleged perpetrator claims to have later observed baby Jesus taking a stroller walk with the sheep in the nursery while the service was concluded."

In talking to my daughter-in-law Heather later on, I learned the real story. They had gone to Heather's parents' church early because Heather's brother was to record the children's program. Vivian joined in with the other children and was allowed to be in the program. She stayed with her parents until it was time to go on stage. According to Heather, Vivian did quite well until it was time to go off stage; she did not want to leave baby Jesus. Heather thought

Vivian stole the baby, but when they watched the video later, they realized that an adult had handed her the baby so she would exit the stage.

Ever since I heard that story, I have thought that we should all be like Vivian in that she wanted to stay close to Jesus. She did not care what others thought or listen to those who were telling her to leave Jesus behind. When she was allowed to take Jesus with her, Vivian consented to leave the stage.

There are many voices in our lives that tell us to leave Jesus behind. When making decisions, we often forget to think about our relationship with Him, only considering our own desires as we make choices. Would we go the places we go, watch the things we watch, or listen to the things we listen to if we truly realized that Jesus is with us in every situation? Or how about the way we treat others? Would it change the way we speak (even when alone) if we sensed the presence of Jesus every time we uttered a word?

As we journey through life, let's make a deliberate choice not to leave Jesus behind as we go about our daily existence. To be truthful, we don't really leave Him behind because He is with us always; we just choose to ignore His presence. Our lives could be so much richer if we hold on to Him and keep aware of Him walking alongside us!

> "Be on your guard so that you are not carried away by the error of unprincipled men and fall from your own steadfastness, but grow in the grace and knowledge of our Lord and Savior Jesus Christ. To Him be the glory, both now and to the day of eternity. Amen" (2 Peter 3:17b-18 NASB).

> "But examine everything carefully; hold fast to that which is good; abstain from every form of evil. Now may the God of peace Himself sanctify you entirely; and may your spirit and soul and body be preserved complete, without blame at the coming of our Lord Jesus Christ. Faithful is He who calls you, and He also will bring it to pass" (1 Thessalonians 5:21-24 NASB).

LUNCH ROBBERS

During my junior year of high school (my sister Terri's sophomore year), her locker was much closer to the school cafeteria than mine was. We decided to put both our lunches in her locker so that we could get to the cafeteria more quickly at lunchtime. Unfortunately, there was a large group of tough kids that hung out around the area where Terri's locker was located. After a few days of putting our lunches in it, they began to turn up missing.

The reason we brought lunches to school in the first place was because our parents did not have the money for us to buy them. When our lunches were stolen, we would go hungry. With no lock to secure the locker, we decided to sabotage our lunches. Actually, on that particular day, we made two sets of lunches. We put the "good" set in my locker, out of the way or not. The doctored set was stashed in Terri's.

Our neighbor up the road did not drive and was all the time having Mom get tobacco for her. Terri and I got the idea of making "tobacco salad" sandwiches (imitation tuna) for our fake lunches. We "borrowed" some of our neighbor's tobacco and mixed it up with mayonnaise and relish and added quite a large amount of onion salt. Then we spread it on bread to make sandwiches. These went into the doctored set of lunches.

When we went to school that day, we nonchalantly put our lunches in Terri's locker just like on any other day. (Of course, the real ones had already been

61

stashed in mine.) Sure enough, when we checked it out at lunchtime, the lunch bags were missing. We have often pictured in our minds the scene of someone eating those lunches. Can you imagine the surprise on their face when they bit into that horrible concoction? Needless to say, no one ever bothered to steal our lunches anymore!

Maybe you have never stolen someone's lunch, but can you honestly say you have never robbed someone of joy or a sense of accomplishment? It is such a temptation to try to be one step higher than another person. We could say, "You did a nice job" or "I am really glad for you." However, our reaction is more like one of these: "I did that quite successfully a while back." "It would have been better if … " "Must be nice!" "Well, almost anyone could have done that!" We convey the feeling that their accomplishment really doesn't have a whole lot of meaning. The person who was looking for someone to share their joy had it stolen instead.

We really haven't meant to rob someone of joy; we have just rattled off whatever popped into our head. We need to watch more closely what we say and consider how it will affect the listener. Often our replies are not well thought out, they are just glib phrases that seem to roll off our tongue and show that either we weren't really listening or that we could not care less.

Let's be more careful in how we listen and especially in how we reply. We don't want to steal someone's joy, nor do we want to bite into something unexpected if we do so!

"Let your conversation be always full of grace, seasoned with salt, so that you may know how to answer everyone" (Colossians 4:6 NIV).

Day 30

DON'T GET TOO COMFORTABLE

You are totally relaxed and ready to fall asleep, or maybe you have already drifted off. Completely comfortable and enjoying every second of it. Then something happens, and you have to shift positions. It may be an itch in the middle of your shoulder blade that just HAS to be scratched. It may be a spouse shifting positions and rearranging the blankets you had so perfectly situated. Now you can feel air space around your feet. Or perhaps your child needs the attention of a parent. The telephone rings. No matter the reason, you reluctantly leave your cozy nest and take care of the problem, even if it just means adjusting the covers. Now it is time to get back to your rest.

Isn't it funny that no matter how you try, you cannot seem to get back into the same comfortable position you had before? You may relax enough to go to sleep, but the "just right" feeling is gone.

Life is so much like this for the Christian. We tend to find our niche and get comfortably settled in. Day after day passes, and we are content with how things are. Then comes the disturbance. Big or small, something occurs to prod us out of our satisfaction and into a period of unrest. We begin to realize that life is not about a comfort zone for us, but a path that will lead us to Heaven. We are in this world but not of it. We are not supposed to be comfortable here. The Lord has His ways of reminding us that we should keep our eyes toward the prize and not on our earthly surroundings. With eternal life as our end goal, we should never be satisfied to view life on earth as our comfort zone.

It reminds me of an old song title: "This World Is Not My Home" ...

> "Therefore if you have been raised up with Christ, keep seeking the things above, where Christ is, seated at the right hand of God. Set your mind on the things above, not on the things that are on earth" (Colossians 3:1-2 NASB).

Day 31

A FITTING PROBLEM

Finding a pair of pants that fit is very frustrating for me. Some people can walk into a store and grab their size, but I am a size that manufacturers seem to ignore. For one thing, I am too tall for a petite size and too short for most misses sizes. If I try on petites, they fit better in the waist and hips, but the hem is at the top of my ankles. (Now, I don't know about you, but where I grew up we would have referred to that hem-length as high-water pants—definitely unacceptable!) The same number size in a Misses will be closer to the correct length (or maybe a little long) but the crotch hangs down way lower than what it should. The solutions I have found are not very good; I either roll the waistband or pull it up around my ribcage. I have tried altering slacks for myself but usually end up worse off than when I started.

Then there is the elastic thing. I do not wear pants that have no "give" in the waistband. My past middle-aged figure is very uncomfortable wearing something snug around my waist. One thing I have learned in my pants-buying expeditions is that the amount of elastic around the waist is not proportional to the size of the pants. I have held up pants of different sizes and found out that they have the same amount of elastic. So now I not only have a crotch that hangs halfway to my knees, but I am being bisected in the middle!

I have tried making pants for myself. I can measure and fit and think I have them right, but when I finish, the pants never seem to fit correctly. I have tried several fitting tricks, such as taking an old pair of pants that fit reasonably well and using them to make a pattern. No matter how hard I try, I never end up with a well-fitting pair of slacks. I have even thought about buying one of the computer programs where you put in detailed measurements, and a pattern is created just for you. However, I read a review about the one of the most popular ones. The common complaint was that it took several "tweaks" to get slacks to fit reasonably well. So much for modern technology!

I was contemplating the fact that my wardrobe is in serious need of help and dreading the thought of trying to find a pair of pants that fit. Then I was struck by the realization that Jesus always fits. He is never too big and impersonal nor is He too small for our greatest need. He never shrinks in the wash nor does He stretch beyond recognition. Favorite clothing can fade with time and fray around the edges, but Jesus is always fully there, never wearing out. He never binds us so tightly that we cannot let go of Him, but His grip on us is firm and sure, giving us the security that we can trust Him come what may. He doesn't sag, bag or leave parts of us that should be covered uncomfortably bare. He is not a fad that will be gone next year, nor is He something we should pack away until the season rolls around again to "wear" Him.

How wonderful to know that no matter where we find ourselves in life, Jesus is the perfect fit!

"For all of you who were baptized into Christ have clothed yourselves with Christ" (Galatians 3:27 NASB).

"For the Scripture says, 'Whoever believes in Him will not be disappointed'" (Romans 10:11 NASB).

Day 32

BEAR OR BARE

Sometimes words can be a hazard to our understanding, especially homonyms. And there is even controversy over the definition of the word "homonym". I learned in school that homonyms are words that sound the same but are spelled differently and have different meanings. But I guess there are those who define them as words that are spelled alike AND sound alike, but have different meanings. The others are called "homophones." Whatever the case, they can cause confusion, especially when one is not sure which word (or spelling) to use.

Take for instance the words "there" (indicating a place), "their" (belonging to them) and they're (a contraction meaning "they are"). I have seen these words misused so many times. Many people use "their" for "they're", as in "their going to the store". Seeing a phrase like "there friends" makes me want to ask, "Do you have 'here friends' as well?" It makes me cringe because I was taught at home and in school that proper usage is important.

I have loved books and reading for as long as I can remember, so it will come as no surprise that I am still an avid reader. I cannot believe the things that make it into print these days; I have to wonder if there is such a thing as an editor anymore. Even if authors choose the wrong word, a decent editor should pick it up. I have seen "brake" used instead of "break" – does a "coffee brake" mean you literally had to stop for coffee? One I recently ran across: "all woks of life". I had not seen "woks" used for "walks" before. I just shook my head.

The words "bear" and "bare" can be extremely troublesome if used in the wrong place and have caused many a chuckle. A headline reading "too much to bare" has a totally different meaning than "too much to bear". The phrases "bearing children" and "baring children" paint word pictures that are SO not the same.

After having said that, I am going to intentionally make a point with these two words.

During a sermon one Sunday, the minister was saying that we "bear His image", meaning that as Christians, we carry the image of Christ. For some reason, another take on the word popped into my head. Our lives should "bare" the image of Christ that we carry with us so that He may be seen instead of us. All too often, we are guilty of wanting to be noticed for our own accomplishments instead of seeking to let Jesus shine on others through a life devoted to demonstrating Him.

As we "bear" the image of Jesus, let's work hard to make sure we "bare" it, too!

> "But we have this treasure in jars of clay to show that this all-surpassing power is from God and not from us. We are hard pressed on every side, but not crushed; perplexed, but not in despair; persecuted, but not abandoned; struck down, but not destroyed. We always carry around in our body the death of Jesus, so that the life of Jesus may also be revealed in our body. For we who are alive are always being given over to death for Jesus' sake, so that his life may also be revealed in our mortal body" (2 Corinthians 4:7-11 NIV).

Day 33

PITY PARTY

My cat Tennyson was a master at feeling sorry for himself. One Saturday I noticed that his right rear leg kept twitching when he was lying down. I picked him up and examined his paw, only to realize that one of the pads was swollen to twice its normal size. Then came a peroxide treatment, which went over like a lead balloon.

On the following Monday, Tennyson underwent a very undesired trip to the veterinarian. He did not care for the ride and meowed his protest all the way there. He was extremely indignant when they took his temperature rectally. When the vet looked at his paw, he struggled to get away. After his diagnosis of an infected pad, Tennyson was glad to get back into the pet carrier. Then he cried all the way home (thank goodness it was just a few blocks!)

Unfortunately for Tennyson, the vet told me to keep up with the peroxide treatment two times a day. There was also a liquid antibiotic to be taken twice a day. I could tell by the smell of it what Tennyson's reaction would be. He did not like it at all, and he would run away when he heard it being shaken up. After he had taken his medicine (protesting all the while), he would give me one of his "Don't you feel sorry for me?" looks. Then he would act very offended with his lot in life.

There are too many times that I get in a mood like Tennyson's and find it hard to see past the hurts and indignities of life. All I seem to want to do is throw a big pity party for myself. However, I know that no one wants to come, so why make the effort? Unlike Tennyson, I realize that this attitude is not what the Lord desires for me. As a teenager, my daughter Molly would be very quick to tell me, "Mom, just GET OVER it!" The funny thing is, Molly didn't want to hear me say that if she was the one giving the pity party. It seems that when we get down in the dumps, more and more things happen to keep us that way. Often it is a lot of piddly little things that add up until they feel like a huge burden.

Have you ever looked at someone else and seen the boulder they have to carry and realized that although they have a boulder, your load of pebbles and stones weighs about the same amount? Then you begin to understand that the major difference is that most of the stones in your load are ones you have picked up yourself. We weigh ourselves down with so much that is unnecessary and when the Holy Spirit reminds us that we are not to fret and worry we just lean down and pick up a few more pebbles. But our God is faithful to His promises, and He will take care of our burdens if we let Him. We need to give God our collection of rocks, and he will give us eternal treasure to take their place.

"Cast your burden upon the Lord and He will sustain you;
He will never allow the righteous to be shaken" (Psalm 55:22 NASB).

"Blessed be the Lord, who daily bears our burden,
The God who is our salvation. Selah" (Psalm 68:19 NASB).

Day 34

SPOOLS

Some of the most versatile "toys" that my sisters and I played with were big wooden spools from electrical wire. My dad was an electrician, and he would bring them home when they became empty. They came in various sizes, and we made use of them all. There was a great big one that made a fine picnic table. Some of the smaller ones were used for stools to sit around it. The medium sized stools were "wheelchairs". We would set them on their sides and roll them with our hands while sitting and scooting on the center.

The stools also came in handy for performances. Three big ones made the three rings for a circus. We used two of them with a board across them to act out The Three Billy Goats Gruff. If we set the biggest one on its side and put bricks under the edges so it would not roll, it only took a long board and we had a seesaw. If the board was propped up just right, we could use it for a slide.

One of our favorite things to do was turn the middle sized ones on their sides and walk on the middles, seeing just how far we could go without falling off. My sister Cindy was a skinny little thing, and she used to wrap herself around the middle of one and get someone to push it to start it rolling. Around and around she would go until the spool stopped or someone stopped it. I am sure we had many more uses for the spools, but those are the ones I can remember easily.

Have you ever stopped and thought about how versatile the Bible is? In this day and age, Christians are often referred to as "Bible thumpers" because we turn to the Scriptures not only for answers to life's questions but for guidance in our everyday lives. Nowhere else we can find such a vast range of resources to meet us exactly where we are in our lives. A certain passage of Scripture can reveal one thing to us in our youth and yet touch us in different ways as we grow older. The actual meaning does not change, just how it fits our lives at that point in time.

The more I study God's Word, the more I realize how comprehensive it is. Praise His Holy Name that He has provided such a wonderful source of strength and comfort, hope and love, and even discipline. He has also provided His Holy Spirit to help us comprehend what we read. Our job is to read – He provides the understanding when we seek Him with all of our hearts.

"Every word of God is flawless;
he is a shield to those who take refuge in him" (Proverbs 30:5 NIV).

"For my thoughts are not your thoughts,
neither are your ways my ways,"
declares the Lord.
As the heavens are higher than the earth,
so are my ways higher than your ways
and my thoughts than your thoughts.
As the rain and the snow
come down from heaven,
and do not return to it
without watering the earth
and making it bud and flourish,
so that it yields seed for the sower and bread for the eater,
so is my word that goes out from my mouth;
it will not return to me empty,
but will accomplish what I desire
and achiever the purpose for which I sent it" (Isaiah 55:8-11 NIV).

"For who among men knows the thoughts of a man except the spirit of the man which is in him? Even so the thoughts of God no one knows except the Spirit of God. Now we have received, not the spirit of the world, but the Spirit who is from God, so that we may know the things freely given to us by God, which things we also speak, not in words taught by human wisdom, but in those taught by the Spirit, combining spiritual thoughts with spiritual words" (1 Corinthians 2:11-13 NASB).

Day 35

GETTING OVER THE HUMP

One of the hardest things about hemming jeans, either to shorten them or to make shorts out of them, is the thick seams. A heavy-duty needle will pierce through them, but the presser foot does not keep an even pressure when sewing through two layers of fabric, then six for a few stitches, and then back down to two. Some wise person invented a little gadget called a Jean-a-ma-jig™, which goes under the presser foot until you get over the hump caused by the thick seam. When you get to the next seam, you just use it again until you have sewn over the hump. Someone else came up with the same type of thing; they called theirs a Hump Jumper®.

There are days in life that we all need a hump jumper – something to get us over the hump and back into the flow of things. It can be a verse or several verses of Scripture, extra time spent in prayer, a special song, or encouragement from someone else. Some days all it takes is a smile from a complete stranger to get our day back into perspective.

We can also act as hump-jumpers for other people although we may never know it at the time. A telephone call, an e-mail, a hug, or even a big smile can brighten someone else's day. Sharing favorite Scriptures that we find helpful can be a real blessing as well.

Let's all look for ways that we can help someone else over a hump! We might even find ourselves repaid during a time when we are in need of assistance.

Here is a favorite Scripture of mine in two different versions:

"Let us not lose heart in doing good, for in due time we will reap if we do not grow weary" (Galatians 6:9 NASB).

"Let us not become weary in doing good, for at the proper time we will reap a harvest if we do not give up" (Galatians 6:9 NIV).

Day 36

LYRICALLY SPEAKING

My children grew up listening to various Christian music artists; one of them was Don Francisco. Besides listening at home, music was usually playing in our car, even on short trips around town. Of course, we just HAD to sing along – that was part of the enjoyment (not to mention worship) of the music.

Have you ever had an "Aha!" moment when you realize the words you happen to be singing are not the correct lyrics to the song? One of my "well, duh!" moments was when I finally comprehended the last few words to "Sheltered in the Arms of God"[1]. "He walks with me and naught of earth shall harm me" made a lot more sense than "not a bird shall harm me." I had never understood why the songwriter would think of birds harming people (unless she had seen the Alfred Hitchcock movie "The Birds").

My middle child had some trouble with lyrics; just enough to make life interesting. He had a different take on Don Francisco's song "Adam, Where Are You?"[2] The words to the song described God walking through the Garden of Eden calling "Adam, Adam, where are you?" What my son Adam actually sang was "Adam, Adam, where is me?"

---

[1]   "Sheltered In the Arms of God" by Dottie Rambo and Jimmie Davis, ©1969 PEERMUSIC LTD

[2]   "Adam, Where Are You" by Don Francisco, ©1977 NEW SPRING PUBLISHING, INC

Listening to that song made me stop and reflect. I thought of how many times God has asked me the question, "Where are you?" Maybe I have started watching a movie that has turned out to have scenes I did not anticipate when I began viewing it, or perhaps been engrossed in a book that takes an unexpected vulgar turn. Maybe I am getting ready to tell a joke that is not one I should be sharing. I might be thinking of doing something I shouldn't or dwelling on things from my past that I wish I had not done.

It may be that God is reminding me that I have been too "busy" to take time to spend with Him in prayer that morning. His gentle voice has a way of drawing me to Him, and He causes me to realize that nothing is as important to me as His love. Finishing an interesting movie or book is not worth feeling stained in my soul. Raunchy jokes are not so funny when compared to what God desires for my life. Where I "am" does not matter nearly as much as where God wants me to be. I will be eternally grateful for God's question, "Where are you?" and pray that I will always be open to hearing it.

> "Those whom I love, I reprove and discipline; therefore be zealous and repent. Behold, I stand at the door and knock; if anyone hears my voice and opens the door, I will come in to him and dine with him, and he with Me. He who overcomes, I will grant to him to sit down with Me on My throne, as I also overcame and sat down with My Father on His throne" (Revelation 3:19-21 NASB).

Day 37

LIFT UP YOUR VOICE

One spring I faced one of the worst allergy seasons I had ever endured. I suffered from itchy eyes, stuffy head, and a tickly throat. When I started to talk I never know what was going to come out– maybe a whisper, maybe a scratchy imitation, or maybe nothing. I managed to startle my granddaughter Maggie, who was three years old at the time, more than once. Just when I got used to forcing out my words so that she could hear me, my voice would suddenly come back. When it did, Maggie thought I was yelling at her. I had to convince her that it was a surprise to me as well! Thankfully, she was okay with that.

Maggie had been to choir practice with us quite a bit that year. She seemed to enjoy being a "part" of the choir during practice. I tried to keep her occupied with coloring or looking at books; she also enjoyed little visits with other members of the choir.

A few days after choir practice one week, I was sitting in my recliner talking to my sister on the telephone. Maggie was playing with toys and came into the living room with her child-size ironing board. She set it up in front of me and then left the room. She came back with a folded sheet of paper and a pencil, stood behind the ironing board facing me, laid the paper on the ironing board, held up the pencil, and told me to sing.

Although quite amused at Maggie's imitation of our choir director, I informed her that my voice was not at its best, so I could not do as she directed. Maggie looked at me expectantly and replied, "That's okay, Grammie, you can just sing a squeaky song!"

As I thought about this little incident, I began to wonder how often God tells us to do something, and we don't do so because we feel inadequate. We neglect to stop and think about the strength we can draw from Him, nor do we consider the fact that He would not ask us to do what He knew we could not handle.

Many times the inadequacies we feel are the result of comparing ourselves with others we think would do a better job. Again, we fail to consider that God did not give the job to someone else; He gave it to us. We are the ones He chooses to accomplish that particular task.

Let's stop trying to second-guess God. He knows what He needs to be done, and He also knows the best person for the job, even if it is singing a "squeaky song". There may be someone who needs to hear it.

> "As each one has received a special gift, employ it in serving one another as good stewards of the manifold grace of God. Whoever speaks, is to do so, as one who is speaking the utterances of God; whoever serves is to do so as one who is serving by the strength which God supplies; so that in all things God may be glorified through Jesus Christ, to whom belongs the glory and dominion forever and ever. Amen" (1 Peter 4:10-12 NASB).

Day 38

PLUG INTO THE POWER!

One year for Christmas, my sister Terri and I received little wooden ironing boards and child-sized irons that actually heated up. Our dad made us a special extension cord so we could plug them in more easily. We ironed lots and lots of doll clothes whenever we played house. One day I was ironing by myself. I plugged in the extension cord and then plugged in my iron and waited for it to heat up. I kept checking it, but my iron never would get warm. I went to my mom, and she came to check out my problem. It seems that I had plugged the iron into one of the outlets on the extension cord, and I had plugged the extension cord itself into the other one! Although this happened during my preschool years, Mom still teased me about it even after I was all grown up.

Have you ever found yourself plugged into the wrong source? It could be your work, your hobbies, your family, or even yourself. When we try to draw strength and power from these places alone, they are bound to fail. God is the only true source of power – if we are not plugged into Him, we will find ourselves wondering why we aren't receiving any energy. We cannot warm up to who we should be unless we are connected to the Giver of Life.

"I pray that the eyes of your heart may be enlightened in order that you may know the hope to which he has called you, the riches of his glorious inheritance in his holy people, and his incomparably great power for us who believe. That power is the same as the mighty strength, he exerted when he raised Christ from the dead and seated him at his right hand in the heavenly realms, far above all rule and authority, power and dominion, and every name that is invoked, not only in the present age but also in the one to come" (Ephesians 1:18-21 NIV).

"I pray that out of his glorious riches he may strengthen you with power through his Spirit in your inner being, so that Christ may dwell in your hearts through faith. And I pray that you, being rooted and established in love, may have power, together with all the Lord's holy people, to grasp how wide and long and high and deep is the love of Christ" (Ephesians 3:16-18 NIV).

"Finally, be strong in the Lord and in his mighty power" (Ephesians 6:10 NIV).

Day 39

FISH FOOD

I belong to a church that celebrates communion every week. Although some say it becomes commonplace, I respectfully beg to differ. To me, it is an important part of worship – a time to reflect on my relationship with my Savior.

During communion time one Sunday, I was waiting for the tray to reach me. I remember listening to the music and thinking the words as the instrumentalists played. The trays our congregation uses have a small bread plate in the center and cups of juice in the outer rings. The plate is usually filled with hard little rectangles of "bread". When I received the tray from the lady sitting next to me, I noticed that things had changed. Instead of rectangles, the bread plate held small white squares that looked like they had been cut from foam packing material.

It is my personal practice to break my "bread" as a symbolic gesture indicating Jesus' broken body. However, this communion wafer would not snap in two, it flexed. When I put it in my mouth, it dissolved before I could even think about chewing it. That is when my memory started kicking in big time. We had goldfish when I was young, and the wafer reminded me of their food. My sisters and I were quite adventurous, and I must admit that we ate some of the flakes to see how they tasted.

So there I sat in church feeling totally irreverent as the thought ran through my head "We are being served fish food for communion!" Guilt began to insert itself into my meditation time. It was then that I sensed a deep belly laugh coming from a Presence that was not of this world. And then I could all but hear a voice asking, "Who do you think gave you your sense of humor?" After the question came a deep awareness of the Lord's presence and His arms around me holding me close to Him. Tears of joy ran down my face as I relished His loving embrace and felt his acceptance of me. And I understood that was what communion is all about – drawing close to Him.

"For as often as you eat this bread and drink the cup, you proclaim the Lord's death until He comes" (1 Corinthians 11:26 NASB).

Day 40

TURN ON YOUR HEADLIGHTS

I was taking the younger two of my children to work at a day camp. It was early in the morning, and I needed to drive about 15 minutes from home to meet the person who would transport them the rest of the way to the camp. Even though the sun was coming out, there was a lot of mist in the air. I turned on my headlights before I even left the driveway. I did not need them to see, but I know that it helps others to see my vehicle if the lights are on. The drive was pretty much through the country even if it was on a state road. Besides the mist, there were some pretty dark clouds overhead as well. As I drove, I noticed that many people had not bothered to turn on their lights and sometimes it was hard to see their vehicles until they were getting really close. The gray vehicles were the hardest to spot—dark ones ran a close second.

My family will tell you that people who drive without headlights in dreary weather are a pet peeve of mine. Granted, they may not need them to see. But it sure helps me to see them! It can get rather scary when a car shows up all of a sudden out of nowhere. To me, it is a courtesy issue as well as one of safety. If I have any doubt about driving conditions, I turn on my lights. And I am grateful to other drivers who do the same thing.

Jesus told us that as His followers, we are the light of the world. However, too many times we are going through life with our headlights turned off! We blend in with our surroundings instead of being a beacon to those traveling the same road we are on, making us unrecognizable to fellow Christians as well as non-believers. We find it much easier to go with the flow than to stand out for all to see. The language of the world is on our lips, and we seek the same forms of entertainment that non-believers choose. We find excuses not to stand out because we do not want to offend other people, or so we say, forgetting that we are offending our Lord in the process.

As I drove that morning, I was thankful for the other drivers that had their headlights turned on. And it means a lot when we meet fellow believers as we journey towards Heaven. If our headlights are shining through the mists of this life, maybe it will remind others to use theirs as well.

Don't forget to turn on your lights!

> "You are the light of the world. A town built on a hill cannot be hidden. Neither do people light a lamp and put it under a bowl. Instead they put it on its stand, and it gives light to everyone in the house. In the same way, let your light shine before others, that they may see your good deeds and glorify your Father in heaven" (Matthew 5:14-16 NIV).

> "He who is not with Me is against Me; and he who does not gather with Me scatters" (Matthew 12: 30 NASB.)

Day 41

GET READY!

One winter day I had an appointment to get my hair cut. While in town, I decided to stop by our local big box store since there were a few things I needed to pick up. A quick shopping trip turned into 2 hours as I battled down the aisles looking for the items on my list. A store that is not usually very busy on a Wednesday morning was full of people stocking up on groceries. I was thankful that I did not have very much in my cart when I went through the checkout lane! And I will admit that a small amount of the two hours was spent browsing through the Christmas clearance aisles, although I did not buy anything from there.

Why was the store so crowded? Everyone wanted to beat the snow that was forecasted for that day (and did happen to fall as predicted). We had heard warnings all week that the weather was coming. Furthermore, it was to be a light, powdery snow – that meant it would drift very easily. Arctic air was supposed to flow through our area the next day, bringing frigid temperatures and winds to cause the drifting. People were getting ready for bad weather conditions.

The Bible tells us to be ready for the return of Jesus. However, we become complacent and fail to keep our souls prepared for His imminent return. After all, people have been watching for Him more than two thousand years. We get so caught up in everyday life that we forget to remember today could be the day. When we wake up in the morning, our mind is full of the things we want to accomplish before we go to bed that night. How many times do we awaken with the thoughts, "Today might be the day of Christ's return! What should I do to make sure I am ready? How can I help others be prepared?" If we focused on those areas, what would change on our "to do" lists?

The concept of eternity gets lost in our attention on the "here and now". When Christ returns, there is so much that will not matter. Things like which team won the ball game. Or if I have read the latest novel from a famous author or seen the most acclaimed movie or played the most recent version of a video game or own the newest computer. What will matter is how we have prepared our souls. Are you ready? He *is* coming– maybe today!

> "Behold, I am coming quickly, and My reward is with Me, to render to every man according to what he has done" (Revelation 22:12 NASB).

> "He who testifies to these things says, "Yes, I am coming quickly." Amen. Come, Lord Jesus" (Revelation 22:20 NASB).

> "But of that day or hour no one knows, not even the angels in heaven, nor the Son, but the Father alone. Take heed, keep on the alert; for you do not know when the appointed time will come" (Mark 13:32-33 NASB).

Day 42

TALKING SCRIPTURES

One year, our Sunday School class started a study of the book of Proverbs on the first day of a month. The teacher suggested it would be beneficial if we read a chapter of Proverbs daily; the one that corresponded with that day's date. We were asked to keep track of anything that "jumped off the page" at us.

In chapter 6, these verses caught my eye:

> "When you walk about, they will guide you;
> When you sleep, they will watch over you;
> And when you awake, they will talk to you.
> For the commandment is a lamp and the teaching is light;
> And reproofs for discipline are the way of
> life" (Proverbs 6:22-23 NASB).

Scripture, if we learn it, really does talk to us. Verses that we may have read over and over before can suddenly take on new meaning for where we are in our lives. The Holy Spirit uses Scripture to convict, to strengthen, and to encourage us. I thought of how I was reading in Luke 6 several days prior to finding the verse in Proverbs. I read verse 46 ("Why do you call Me, 'Lord, Lord,' and do not do what I say?" NASB) and started to keep on reading when the Holy Spirit spoke to me and said, "This verse is for you."

Now I don't know about anyone else, but I have associated this verse with people who claim to know Jesus, but their actions declare otherwise. Or people who assume that just because they go to church they are Christians. Or Scribes and Pharisees. Or whoever else. Just not me. After all, I am trying to be what God would have me be. I know I have a long way to go, but I am learning and growing and becoming. So why this verse for me?

And then other verses began to come to mind:

> "So do not worry about tomorrow; for tomorrow will care for itself" (Matthew 6:34 NASB).

> "If then you cannot do even a very little thing, why do you worry about other matters? ... do not keep worrying" (Luke 12:26,29b NASB).

> "Be anxious for nothing" (Philippians 4:6a NASB).

I know that worry is a big problem for me; I struggle with getting it out of my life. I must admit, though, that my struggle has often been half-hearted. I feel like I don't know how to let go. And to be truthful, I think I am afraid to let go ...

Scripture begins talking again ...

> "Do not let your heart be troubled, nor let it be fearful." (John 14:27b NASB).

> "There is no fear in love; but perfect love casts out fear" (1 John 4:18a NASB).

> "Do not fear, for I am with you;
> Do not anxiously look about you, for I am your God.
> I will strengthen you, surely I will help you,
> Surely I will uphold you with My righteous
> right hand" (Isaiah 41:10 NASB).

"Do not fear, for I have redeemed you;
I have called you by name; you are Mine!" (Isaiah 43:1b NASB).

As God's Word began to convict my heart, I realize that I need to stop trying and start letting Him be in control of removing worry and fear from my mind. My efforts often hamper what He wants to do. And that is why that verse is for me.

Lest anyone get the wrong idea that I remember all the Scripture references as well as the verses, I will say this: A good concordance is a wonderful tool!

A LESSON FROM OKRA PLANTS

One of the favorite things I plant in my garden is okra. I like it pan fried, deep fried, stewed with corn and tomatoes, added to gumbo soup, pickled … actually, I haven't discovered a way that I don't like it.

The first year after we moved to the country, my husband and I planted a big garden. We had never planted okra before, and as it came up I soon realized that the plants were much too close together. Okra plants grow quite large, so I knew that they needed to be thinned out. The hardest part for me was pulling up healthy plants. I understood that the ones remaining needed room to grow and spread out, but I felt like a murderer when I tugged up the others.

Since there was an empty space in the row next to the okra, I decided that it could not hurt to try transplanting the ones I would otherwise discard. I would at least give them a fighting chance; if they died, I was out nothing because they would have died anyway. If they lived, we stood to have a more abundant harvest.

My daughter Molly and I worked together to put the little okra plants back into the ground. We watered them well, wondering whether or not they would survive. After a few days, they looked pathetic; however, it was not long before a transformation took place. As their roots began to develop, the plants began to green up and soon they looked healthy again. Although they were slower to produce than the first row of okra, they definitely added to our harvest!

As Christians, we often get involved in more than we can do and do well. It is so easy to agree to do things we know that we are capable of doing. If not careful, we find ourselves meeting ourselves coming and going. Even though we may be doing good things, we sacrifice doing our best for doing too much. I find that for me, it is hard to relinquish something that I have been doing because I know that it needs to be done. I think that someone else may not do it in a manner that suits me. Not that I am the one to set the standard; it is just hard for me to let go.

When I watched the "new" row of okra developing, I began to realize that God will provide ways for jobs to be done in His Kingdom. I need to cultivate those tasks that are best for me and learn to let Him take care of the rest. It can be interesting to see where the "discarded" plants will take root. They may not grow in the same way for someone else as they did for me, but that is okay. God can better use me when I concentrate on doing fewer things in a more excellent manner than when I do lots of things in a mediocre fashion. When I keep a grasp on things I need to give up, I may be preventing someone else from doing something they are better suited for than I am.

> "Now there are varieties of gifts, but the same Spirit. And there are varieties of ministries, and the same Lord. There are varieties of effects, but the same God who works all things in all persons. But to each one is given the manifestation of the Spirit for the common good ... But now God has placed the members, each one of them, in the body just as He desired. If they were all one member, where would the body be? But now there are many members, but one body" (1 Corinthians 12:4-7, 18-20 NASB).

> "Those who have served well gain an excellent standing and great assurance in their faith in Christ Jesus" (1 Timothy 3:13 NIV).

Day 44

BUT THAT IS WHAT I WANTED ...

The year I was in second grade, I told my parents that I wanted a Santa Claus doll for Christmas. My mom and dad tried to talk me out of it, showing me many other dolls that were available. But I insisted that the Santa doll was what I really wanted. I would not change my mind, no matter what they said or how many other dolls there were to be had. On Christmas morning, I was elated to find my Santa doll under our Christmas tree. I played with it all during Christmas vacation.

The day we went back to school, we were allowed to bring our favorite gift for show and tell. By this time, no Christmas decorations were left at home or at school. Christmas was over. I cannot begin to tell you how out of place I felt with my Santa doll. All the other children in my class had brought toys they could play with all year round. But I had a toy that really needed to be boxed up with the rest of the Christmas decorations. My classmates could not believe that anyone would really want a Santa doll for a gift. At home, my sisters had dolls that they could have fun with at any time of the year while mine was out of season. Although my parents had tried to convince me that I really did not want what I asked for, I refused to listen. I wanted what I wanted, and that was that. I was looking at the short term and not thinking about how I would feel about having a Santa doll once Christmas was over.

How often do we tell our Heavenly Father what we desire for our lives, and then expect Him to provide it? We insist on having things our way, and if it does not happen, then we feel that God is punishing us. However, we need to stop and realize that He knows what we really need; even what we really want. His ways are far different than what we can comprehend. And He is always looking at the big picture that we cannot see. I think there are times that God lets us have what we think we want just to prove to us that He really does know best. When we are disappointed, God is there to soothe the hurt. He wraps His loving arms around us and asks, "Will you trust Me now? I really do have your best interest at heart."

"By day the Lord directs his love,
at night his song is with me –
a prayer to the God of my life" (Psalm 42:8 NIV).

"Many, Lord, my God,
are the wonders you have done,
the things you planned for us.
None can compare with you;
were I to speak and tell of your deeds,
they would be too many to declare" (Psalm 40:5 NIV).

Day 45

LOOKING GOOD

Have you ever had an outfit of clothing that really looks good on you? One that whenever you wear it you get lots of compliments, even after you have had it for quite a while? Whenever you wear it, you are confident that you are looking your best. Outfits like that seem to be few and far between, but it is a real blessing to possess one!

While reading in Psalms, I found an "outfit" that is becoming to all God's children – praise. Here is the verse in the NASB: "Sing for joy in the Lord, O you righteous ones; Praise is becoming to the upright" (Psalm 33:1).

I was so intrigued by this that I decided to look it up in some other versions. The NIV states the last part of the verse: "it is fitting for the upright to praise him." So our "outfit" is well-fitting in addition to being becoming.

The next version I looked in was the NKJV, where I found it stated this way: "For praise from the upright is beautiful." We look our very best when we are praising our Creator. The KJV reads: "for praise is comely for the upright." Our praise not only looks good on us, but its ultimate purpose is to glorify God. We attract others to Him when we wear our garment of praise.

Sara Ray

The last version I checked in was the RSV: "Praise befits the upright." It is right for us to look good in our "outfit" of praise. We should wear it often!

> "Praise the Lord!
> For it is good to sing praises to our God;
> For it is pleasant and praise is becoming" (Psalm 147:1 NASB).

Day 46

MEANDERING STREAM

Don't you just love real estate ads? The one for our country property listed several drawing cards: a peony-lined drive, new this and that, and so on and so forth, all bordered by a meandering stream. We have since chuckled about the stream. It is a drainage ditch and referred to as such in the legal description of the property. For several months after we purchased our home, the ditch had been dry. In late winter, after the snow had melted, there began to be puddles in it. The puddles were followed by a slow trickle, with probably an inch or two of water flowing. That was what the "stream" looked like on a Thursday. Then it began to rain, and rain hard. The next morning there was quite a bit of water rushing through the ditch, and it kept getting deeper and deeper and flowing faster and faster. I looked out at it the following Saturday morning, and it had gone down quite a bit. By Sunday, it had slowed to a steady flow; much closer to its real estate portrayal as a meandering stream.

As I walked along the fence above the flowing water, I began to compare that stream to life. There are times we feel all dried up. The evidence is there, however, to prove we have not always been that way - sometimes that evidence is what keeps us going. We know that God has not forsaken us even though we cannot seem to sense His presence. Then something happens to revive us. Our frozen hearts melt and puddles of joy began to form. Showers of blessing become torrents of the abundance of our Heavenly Father, causing a great outpouring of praise and worship from our once-thirsty souls. But we cannot always run at flood stage; life has a way of becoming more normal again. Then we reach the steady flow stage, which is the one that takes us through every day.

The flood stage and the normal, everyday, run-of-the-mill routine are what leave the evidence of the stream. During a dry spell, all we have to do is look at the evidence to see that the water has been there, and we can be assured that it will flow again in time. And the flood stage is made even fuller through the knowledge that we have held on to our faith through the spiritual drought.

> "O God, You are my God; I shall seek You earnestly;
> My soul thirsts for You, my flesh yearns for You,
> In a dry and weary land where there is no water" (Psalm 63:1 NASB).

> "Your righteousness, God, reaches to the heavens,
> you who have done great things.
> Who is like you, God?
> Though you have made me see troubles,
> many and bitter,
> you will restore my life again;
> from the depths of the earth you will again bring me up.
> You will increase my honor and comfort me once more.
> I will praise you with the harp
> for your faithfulness, my God,
> I will sing praise to you with the lyre,
> Holy One of Israel.
> My lips will shout for joy
> when I sing praise to you –
> I whom you have delivered" (Psalm 71:19-23 NIV).

Day 47

OUT OF PLACE TRASH

My son Adam had a cat named Zeke. I found myself aggravated at Zeke a lot. He had an affinity for turning over trash receptacles. He loved to pick out candy wrappers, paper wads, and other things he could carry around in his mouth. One time I scolded my kids for leaving gum wrappers all over the place, only to find out that Zeke had discovered them in the trash and carried his finds throughout the house.

I tried my best to make sure that Zeke never saw me toss it out anything he was prone to play with. I knew that if his watchful golden eyes spotted something going into the trash, he would wait until I was out of the room and then I would hear the THUD! of an overturning wastebasket. Zeke would find what he was seeking and parade around the house with it dangling from his mouth. Occasionally, he would drop it and play with it – then he would pick it up and carry it around some more. When he finally lost interest, he would leave his "treasure" wherever it happened to fall. There were many times that I puzzled over the fact that I thought I had thrown something away, only to have it reappear. Then I would realize that I was not going crazy, I *did* throw it away, but Zeke dug it out of the trash.

There are people in this world that thrive on other people's trash. Slander and gossip are as much a part of their lives as eating. They love to ferret out things that have been forgiven and forgotten by the parties involved and bring them out into public view. Sadly enough, these people can even be found in the church. Some individuals feel that it is their responsibility to warn others about certain people. They may not have all the facts; it is entirely possible that they don't have anything substantial to go by at all. A hint of something out of the norm is all they need to create a credulous story to spread around.

Misjudged motives are an integral part of the whispers from a "trash-picker". It is easy to decide why someone did something based on our own thinking. What we don't know is that person's reason for doing what they did. The motive might have been well-intended, but the outcome was not well thought out. Or maybe things did not end up turning out the way the person had hoped. Many times, the individual realizes that he/she made a mistake and wants forgiveness, but the wastebasket gets turned over and dumped out before it can be emptied.

I find two lessons here. The first one: each one of us needs to make sure that we are not a "trash-picker". If we have a tendency to gossip and to misjudge the motives of others, it is time to ask the Spirit of God to cleanse our lives of that trait. We need to watch what we say about others, even if we think it is well-intentioned. The second lesson: we need to keep our lives as free from sin as possible so that when the trash-pickers are digging through wastebaskets, they will come up empty-handed when they go through ours.

> "Who are you to judge someone else's servant? To their own master, servants stand or fall. And they will stand, for the Lord is able to make them stand. ... You, then, why do you judge your brother or sister? Or why do you treat them with contempt? For we will all stand before God's judgement seat" (Romans 14:4, 10 NIV).

> "In everything set them an example by doing what is good" (Titus 2:7a NIV).

Day 48

THIS WILL HURT ME
MORE THAN YOU

One of the phrases parents use just before meting out punishment on their offspring is, "This is going to hurt me worse than it hurts you." When you are the person up for a spanking, you have to wonder who in the world your parent is trying to fool. Especially when your mother has a willow switch in her hand that is going to sting the dickens out of your backside! My childhood home had two great big weeping willow trees in the front yard, and my mother took advantage of their presence.

After I became a parent, I understood what my parents meant by their statement. It is hard to look into precious little faces and know that you need to take measures to protect them by teaching them not to do wrong. It would be easier to let the situation go and not give punishment, but in your heart you realize that the child will be better off in the long run for learning to obey. I have seen way too many parents who do not discipline themselves to discipline their children, and then they wonder why they have self-centered children.

When Jesus chose the road to Calvary, the punishment for our sin definitely hurt Him worse than it hurt us. He suffered great pain and agony and allowed Himself to be separated from His Father so that we could be a part of His eternal family. He became sin for us so that we might know His glory; all we have to do is accept the sacrifice. He willingly gave Himself for us because He loves us.

Although we are a new creation in Christ, we still mess up. Jesus' sacrifice covers our sin, but it does not take away all the consequences of that sin. And like any good parent, God disciplines us along life's way so that we will remain in Him. We can choose to rebel – He gives us that freedom – however, we are better off to heed His discipline and learn from our mistakes. Sometimes I feel like I can hear Him say, "Sara, I am sorry that you did not do what you were supposed to. I had something much better planned, but you chose this path and now you have to deal with the consequences of your actions." It makes me sad to think that my actions hurt the heart of my Savior. It also gives me the incentive to try harder to listen and learn from Him, to look to Him for guidance in my decisions, and to stay on the path that He has set for my feet. After all, the punishment really did hurt Him worse than it does me.

> "'My son, do not regard lightly the discipline of the Lord,
> Nor faint when you are reproved by Him;
> For those whom the Lord loves He disciplines,
> And He scourges every son whom He receives.'
> It is for discipline that you endure; God deals with you as with
> sons; for what son is there whom his father does not discipline?
> But if you are without discipline, of which all have become
> partakers, then you are illegitimate children and not sons.
> Furthermore, we had earthly fathers to discipline us,
> and we respected them; shall we not much rather
> be subject to the Father of spirits and live?
> For they disciplined us for a short time as seemed
> best to them, but He disciplines us for our good,
> so that we may share in His holiness.
> All discipline for the moment seems not to be joyful, but sorrowful;
> yet to those who have been trained by it, afterwards it yields the
> peaceful fruit of righteousness" (Hebrews 12:5b-11 NASB).

LESSONS FROM A COAT CLOSET

I had never had the pleasure of having a coat closet until we moved to a house in the country. It was so nice to be able to have a place not only for coats, but also for the vacuum cleaner, a toolbox, light bulbs, a broom, and various other items that need to be kept close at hand but out of sight.

When we first moved, our son Jonathan was living with his grandparents while he was attending Ivy Tech. He helped us move, but he hadn't learned all the "details" about our house. I remember the first time he came home for a visit after it was cold enough to wear a coat. Jonathan twisted the knob of the closet door, and it wouldn't open. He twisted harder. Frustration laced his voice as he called out, "Mom, why is the coat closet locked?"

What Jonathan did not know was that the doorknob set was made especially for closets. It latched when you closed it, but all you had to do was pull the knob to open it. All his twisting and turning did absolutely no good because the knob wasn't meant to be turned in the first place. If he had just pulled on it, the door would have opened easily.

As I thought about this story, it came to my mind that we often do the same thing with God. We try to make something difficult out of something easy. He tells us to knock and the door will be opened. But we twist the knob and shake the door and try every other way we can to get it open. "After all," we think, "God should require more than a simple tug at the door." So we do everything we can conceive of until we wear ourselves out enough to decide to follow God's directions. We knock. Why are we so surprised when the door opens?!

Another lesson from the closet: In our coat closet, there are garments for physical warmth. Behind God's door, there is warmth for our souls. We have a vacuum cleaner, dust cloths, and a broom in our closet. God has cleansing for our hearts in His. We have light bulbs in ours; on the other side of His door God has the Light of the World. There is a toolbox in our closet, full of things used to construct and repair. When God opens his door to us, we discover the Maker of all things and the Mender of broken hearts.

"Ask, and it will be given to you; seek, and you will find; knock, and it will be opened to you. For everyone who asks receives, and he who seeks finds, and to him who knocks it will be opened" (Matthew 7:7-8 NASB).

"Therefore the Lord longs to be gracious to you,
And therefore He waits on high to have compassion on you.
For the Lord is a God of justice;
How blessed are all those who long for Him.
… He will surely be gracious to you at the sound of your cry; when he hears it, He will answer you" (Isaiah 30:18, 19b NASB).

Day 50

ARE YOU A MISSING PIECE?

There were a lot of cold winter days when my family would decide to work on a jigsaw puzzle. We sorted the pieces out by color and picked out the edges and corners, putting the "frame" together first. Then we worked at the puzzle off and on until it was finished. Sometimes one piece would be missing from a certain part of the puzzle. First one of us and then another would pick up a piece that looked as if it might fit, trying to find the one that went in the hole. There were many times that the piece we needed did not look as if it would be the right one. It was really frustrating to get a puzzle almost complete, only to realize that one piece was missing entirely. It left us with a feeling of incompleteness.

We are all pieces of the entire picture of God's kingdom. No one else can take our place. We are created as unique individuals. When we go missing no one else can fill our space. Other pieces might look as if they would fit, but they are never quite right. They cannot fill the void we leave when we choose not to be in the picture.

There are times when we feel that we do not belong or that we have been missing for too long. But think of how satisfying it is to find the one missing piece of a jigsaw puzzle and put it into place. The picture is complete instead of having an empty spot. Now the focal point is the whole scene instead of the hole where there was supposed to be a one-of-a-kind piece.

Is your piece missing from God's puzzle? If so, it is time to get back in the picture! You have not been gone too long or changed too much to fit your space. It is still there, a perfect spot, and you will blend right in. All of us need YOU to complete the picture!

"Now you are the body of Christ, and each of you is a part of it" (1 Corinthians 12:27 NIV).

"From him the whole body, joined and held together by every supporting ligament, grows and builds itself up in love, as each part does its work" (Ephesians 4:16 NIV).

Day 51

FOLLOWING A RECIPE

Anyone who knows me very well at all knows that I love to cook. I love to try new recipes, but I do not always follow them as they are written. Several years ago, I answered an ad in the local newspaper – they wanted to interview people who baked Christmas cookies. When the reporter came to our house, she discovered my husband Bob's definition of his wife's cooking: "She takes a recipe and departs therefrom." I must admit, that is quite a true statement.

Rarely do I follow a recipe just like it is written. Sometimes I may not have exactly what the recipe calls for, so I will substitute something else – either that, or leave it out if it is not an essential ingredient. Other times, I think, "I'll bet this would give that recipe a good flavor." So I add in whatever ingredient it is. And then there are times when all I get from the recipe is the general idea. By the time I am finished with it, no one would ever realize that I used that certain recipe to concoct the end product. My family is very used to being experimented with, and fortunately for them, I am usually pretty successful at creating tasty meals.

Unfortunately, many church people try to do with the Scriptures what I do when I follow a recipe. Don't like something? Try something else instead. Or leave it out entirely. Think God's Word would be more palatable if it had this? Add it in. Or how about a pinch of that? Put it in, too. Maybe we should change half of this to some of that? Okay, let's try it. What if we try beating this together instead of gently folding in these ingredients? Might work. Want to cook this at a higher temperature so that it will get done faster? Well, we could get finished and clean up sooner …

I could go on and on, but I think you get what I am trying to say. By the time people get through adding this, subtracting that, and doing this instead of that, the church looks totally unrecognizable when compared to the recipe that God gave us in His Word. What works in my kitchen does not work in the Body of Christ. When we try to change what has been given us by the Master Chef, all we do is create an unpalatable mess. Our Lord knows how to run His kitchen: we need to follow His recipe.

> "Every word of God is tested;
> He is a shield to those who take refuge in Him.
> Do not add to His words
> Or He will reprove you, and you will be proved
> a liar" (Proverbs 30:5-6 NASB).

> "You shall not add to the word which I am commanding you, nor take away from it, that you may keep the commandments of the Lord your God which I command you" (Deuteronomy 4:2 NASB).

> "Whatever I command you, you shall be careful to do; you shall not add to nor take away from it" (Deuteronomy 12:32 NASB).

Day 52

GEORGE SIMPKINS

My sister Terri and I never got along very well when we were growing up. I was the oldest child of six and Terri came next. In my childish view of things I was the slave in the family and she was the pampered princess. I am sure she felt very differently. We used to do things just to aggravate each other, sometimes even getting our younger siblings to be either on her side or on mine. It is a wonder that our mom survived.

One of the things Terri did that I detested most was to tell my mother that I had a crush on any boy she saw me chatting with. Either that or she would decide that the boy had a crush on me. In this game, all the siblings were on her side. If we were all together in the car, they would see boys on the street and yell out of their windows "Sara loves you!" I would always duck down so they could not see me, even though we usually had no clue as to who the boys were. My sister Cindy started calling me Amazing Grace because she said I amazed all the boys on our school bus. (My middle name just happens to be Grace.) The worst part was that I was always painfully shy, and I hated all the attention.

There was one particular day of my senior year of high school that I love to remember. I was in the school library and was working on homework during a study period. Our high school was made up of several round "pods" that were connected by hallways. The library was recessed out of one of the hallways, with bookshelves on one side and study tables across the hall. There were also a few tables on the shelf side of the hall, and that is where I was sitting. I was working with a boy from one of my classes, dreading the thought of Terri spotting me if she came down the hallway. Sure enough, I looked up at one point and there she was. She came over to the table and asked for his name. For some reason, he would not tell her. And, of course, I was not going to give her that information!

I thought my goose was cooked when I saw one of the Social Studies teachers coming down the hall. Terri knew the teacher, and she had no qualms about asking him the boy's name. The teacher took one look at him, told Terri "George Simpkins" and kept right on walking. Whatever possessed him to do so I will never know, but I will be forever grateful. Terri went home that afternoon and told Mom that I was in love with George Simpkins, and the teasing began. But my family got quite a different reaction than what they were expecting. Instead of being mortified, I was doubled over laughing! "George Simpkins" (in this case) was only a product of the teacher's quick wit, not a real person.

Circumstances that we face in life can often be very hurtful. Sometimes we want to crawl into a hole and not come out until they are gone. We have to deal with people when we would like for them just to go away and leave us alone. Even though we realize that we should not withdraw from our surroundings, it would be easy to do so.

In the middle of trials, our wonderful Father God supplies hilarious moments - things to help us make it through the difficulty we are facing. Hardships become much easier to deal with after a good belly laugh! The trouble itself may not change, but our perspective of it does. And the Lord uses the pain and the laughter in our lives to help us be a blessing to others. Later on in life when we look back at that period of our life, we remember the chuckles more so than the pain, the blessings more than the burdens.

> Thank you, God, for tears of laughter!
> "Our mouths were filled with laughter,
> our tongues with songs of joy.
> Then it was said among the nations,
> "The Lord has done great things for them."
> The Lord has done great things for us,

and we are filled with joy …
Those who sow with tears
will reap with songs of joy.
Those who go out weeping,
carrying seed to sow,
will return with songs of joy,
carrying sheaves with him" (Psalm 126:2-3, 5-6 NIV).

Day 53

AN APPLE PIE DAY

One Sunday afternoon I found energy I did not know I had. Adam and Molly (the younger two of my three children) had been home for fall break, but they were headed back to college that evening. The Friday before, Molly and I had been to the orchard to pick apples, and apple pie was sounding really good. I made two batches of crust, and my husband helped me peel the apples. We ended up with five pies. Adam and Molly took one back to school with them, one went in the freezer for my father-in-law, and Adam's girlfriend took one home with her. That left us with two. Needless to say, we ate most of one of them! Jonathan (my oldest child) took the last one to work with him the next morning.

At the time, Jonathan worked in the computer department of a factory that was a small part of a larger corporation. They also had a factory in Mexico City. There was a man from Mexico City working with the facility in Indianapolis the day Jonathan took the pie to work. This man had never tasted apple pie before. According to Jonathan, when the man took his first bite, his eyes lit up, and he remarked, "So *this* is apple pie!"

I told the story to a friend of mine. She commented that she thought it wonderful that the man's first experience with apple pie was with a homemade one instead of one from a grocery store. Her observation caused me to think not only about how we who call ourselves Christians present Jesus to others, but also about the wonderful feeling that we experience when we see Jesus working in our lives.

To many people, Jesus is nothing but a swear word. They have never known the true Son of God. As a Christian, I would pray that my witness of His life in mine would be such that when I show Jesus to them that He would be real and compelling. I want them to know who He really is; I want to be the catalyst that introduces a reaction between Him and them.

I wonder how many times I have failed to show the real Jesus because I am so caught up in my own agenda instead of following His leading in my life. How many times have I been so busy doing good that I fail to do what is best ...

Lord, please forgive me for the times when I get in the way of You shining through me. Help my life to show others the *real* You.

> "Let your light shine before men in such a way that they may see your good works, and glorify your Father who is in heaven" (Matthew 5:16 NASB).

> "Now to Him who is able to do far more abundantly beyond all that we ask or think, according to the power that works within us, to Him be the glory in the church and in Christ Jesus to all generations forever and ever. Amen" (Ephesians 3:20-21 NASB).

ON PAINFUL THINGS

During the last seven years of his life my dad was confined to a wheelchair; rheumatoid arthritis was the culprit. His knees were in a permanently bent position. Because his hands were also misshapen, my mom had to do almost everything for him. He could feed himself if she cut up his food into bite-sized pieces, but there wasn't much else he was able to accomplish. When Dad's knees first started drawing up into their bent positions, the doctors and therapists urged him to exercise them. They told Dad to keep motion in his knees so that they would not freeze in place

At first, Dad seemed to want to keep his knees from locking up. He did the exercises even though they were painful; however, he grew weary of trying and so he did them less and less often. Finally, he gave up on the exercises altogether, and his knees stayed bent. His lack of effort affected not only him but also my mom and the rest of the family.

Sometimes the things we need to do in our Christian walk are painful but necessary to keep us moving ahead. It is not always easy to reach out to others when your efforts have been rejected previously. It is hard to make yourself get in touch with someone and ask for forgiveness; it can be just as hard to be the forgiver. When you lose a close friend to death or distance (physical) it is difficult to build a relationship with someone else. You know how painful loss can be; you do not want to place yourself in a vulnerable position again. However, we may be called to do all these painful things and many more as we go throughout life. Let's make sure we do our "exercises" so that we will not become a burden to others as well as ourselves.

"Therefore we do not lose heart. Though outwardly we are wasting away, yet inwardly we are being renewed day by day. For our light and momentary troubles are achieving for us an eternal glory that far outweighs them all. So we fix our eyes not on what is seen, but on what is unseen, since what is seen is temporary, but what is unseen is eternal" (2 Corinthians 4:16-18 NIV).

Day 55

HAWAIIAN MEATBALLS

I was preparing lunch one day and wanted to fix something that we had not eaten for a while. When I was searching through the refrigerator and cabinets, I realized that we had all the ingredients available for Hawaiian Sweet and Sour Meatballs. As I was working on mixing up the meatballs, I was reminded of a time our Sunday School Class was asked to prepare meals for the family of one of the members during her recovery from surgery. I signed up for the Sunday meal. Not really knowing the family very well, I was unsure of what to fix. I decided to pray for inspiration. While browsing through various recipes, I came across the one for Hawaiian Meatballs. For some reason, it said, "Fix me! Fix me!" and when I went to the grocery store I bought the necessary ingredients.

Later that week, my husband asked me what I was taking to the family for their meal. When I told him, he was very skeptical. "Not everybody likes fruit with their meat," he remarked. (The recipe has pineapple in the sauce that goes over the meatballs.) He thought I should make something a little less "different" than the meatballs. So I prayed even harder about it. "Lord, what should I do? Bob made a valid point." I still felt that the recipe was the right one to fix for this family.

On the following Sunday, we delivered the meal to the lady's husband at church that morning. When I told him what I had prepared, he informed me that she loved pineapple in about anything. And later on, they both told me how much their family had enjoyed that meal. Needless to say, I was vastly relieved that I had not made a big mistake. I was in awe of the way God worked in my choice of what to cook for someone else's meal.

God touches our lives in so many ways. Was it frivolous for me to ask Him what to prepare for another family? Somehow, I don't think so. I believe He answered my prayer and helped me to realize He had answered it even in the face of opposition. (And I am not saying that Bob should not have questioned my decision. His point of view was important to me. I did not ignore it, I just prayed harder to make sure of the answer.) We should never hesitate to pray about even the smallest decisions we have to make. God is not burdened by what we perceive as petty problems. He enjoys helping us solve them, and He strengthens our faith when we see His answers.

> "To You I lift up my eyes,
> O You who are enthroned in the heavens!
> Behold, as the eyes of servants look to the hand of their master,
> As the eyes of a maid to the hand of her mistress,
> So our eyes look to the Lord our God
> Until He is gracious to us" (Psalm 123:1-2 NASB).

Day 56

I TRIED NOT TO GOOF UP, BUT ...

Have you ever tried not to make a mistake, to make sure that you are doing something right, and flubbed up anyway? That has happened to me all too often. Several years ago, I had an appointment with an allergist–my first one. The nurse in our doctor's office had set up the appointment for me. I would not have even known about it had I not gone with my husband to his appointment the week before. (He is battling high cholesterol and the doctor wanted to discuss it with us.) The nurse handed me a slip of paper with the information about my appointment with the allergist. She told me that she had left a message on the answering machine that morning, but thought she would give it to me on paper as well since we were coming to the office. The only problem was that I had been home all morning, and the phone had not rung. I questioned her about it and found out that even though the doctor's office had changed our address and telephone number in the computer records, they had not changed it on my chart. After I had arrived back home, I began to wonder if she had given the wrong information to the allergist's office as well. There was a telephone number on the paper, so I called it just to make sure they had the correct information. The person who answered the telephone did not seem to want to listen to my explanation. She took my address and telephone number because I told her that they might have the wrong ones. However, she acted like it was no big deal.

On the day I went to the allergist's office, one of the first things they asked me was the last time I had taken my allergy medication. Since I did not know to do differently, I had taken it that morning. The trial skin tests did not have any effect, so they tried injecting the allergens under my skin. That worked, so they did all the tests that way. My arms looked like I was a junkie; they were full of needle pricks. It would have been a lot less painful for me if I had known not to take my medicine!

And what do you think was in the mail when I got home? A letter from the allergist's office, telling me not to take any allergy medication for seven days prior to my appointment. It was forwarded from our old address. Even though I had tried to make sure about taking medicine before my appointment, I did not succeed in getting the information that I needed. And with all the pollens that in the air at the time, I didn't want to skip my medicine unless it was necessary for me to do so.

It seems that no matter how hard we try to live perfect lives that honor our Savior, we are always flubbing up. Many times we don't even realize that we have gotten out of step with Jesus until we find ourselves in the middle of a mess. We would have avoided it if we had seen it coming, but we were too busy looking around to watch where we were going. Sometimes it is a matter of taking someone else's word instead of looking to Christ for the answer. We rely on fellow Christians to look out for us and advise us, forgetting that they, too, end up in the middle of messes without realizing it. And getting out of the mess is a far more painful process than avoiding it would have been in the first place.

I don't know what else I could have done to find out the procedure I should have followed before my allergist appointment, but I do know where to find the proper guidance for my life. And when I goof up, I know where to find someone to get me out of the mess and back into the swing of things. God is always ready to take the hand that I hold out to Him for help.

Scripture:

> "For I know that nothing good dwells in me, that is, in my flesh; for the willing is present in me, but the doing of the good is not. For the good that I want, I do not do; but I practice the very evil that I do not want. But if I am doing the very thing I do not want, I am no longer the one doing it, but sin which dwells in me. I find then the

principle that evil is present in me, the one who wants to do good. For I joyfully concur with the law of God in the inner man, but I see a different law in the members of my body, waging war against the law of my mind, and making me a prisoner of the law of sin which is in my members. Wretched man that I am! Who will set me free from the body of this death? Thanks be to God through Jesus Christ our Lord!" (Romans 7:18-25a NASB).

Day 57

DRIVING

God has a way of revealing things in our lives that are sinful. It may not be something that affects anyone else – we cannot point to someone and say that the same thing is sinful for them because we do not know why there is that problem in their life.

For several years after my marriage, I had a terrible fear of driving, and I had to depend on someone else to take me where I needed to go. Then one day I realized that for me, not being able to drive was a sin in my life – it showed my lack of trust in God's ability to take care of me. After much prayer and with a lot of determination, I finally decided I needed to get over my fear.

Our car had a manual transmission, so not only did I have to learn to drive, I had to be coordinated enough to change gears. All was going pretty well until we traded cars. Our new car had a much stiffer transmission than the other one, and it took me a while to get used to it. The passengers in the car would get all shaken up as I tried to get it going again after coming to a stop. I remember one particular day I was having a great deal of trouble pulling out of a country road onto a state highway. I managed to kill the engine every time I tried to go forward. The car kept jerking whenever I started to accelerate. I kept on trying until finally I heard giggles erupting from the back seat where three-year-old Jonathan was fastened into his seat belt. Finally, I managed to get moving again.

I did not give up; I kept on working at it until I received my driver's license. I was twenty-seven years old at the time. When I realized that it was a lack of trust in God that kept me from learning to drive, it dawned on me that the lack of trust was a sin in my life. I knew it was time to step out in faith and deal with my problem. I still am not overly fond of driving, and I detest heavy traffic even if I am a passenger in the car. If I get panicky while driving, I ask the Lord to put His capable hands over mine on the steering wheel. And He does.

That is my story of something that was sinful for me. It took God's revelation to help me realize that it was a problem. I am sure there are things in each one of our lives that we need to deal with. I am most grateful to God that as He shows us what they are, He gives us the strength to work through them.

> "Come and hear, all you who fear God;
> let me tell you what he has done for me.
> I cried out to him with my mouth;
> his praise was on my tongue.
> If I had cherished sin in my heart,
> the Lord would not have listened;
> but God has surely listened and has heard my prayer.
> Praise be to God,
> who has not rejected my prayer
> or withheld his love from me!" (Psalm 66:16-20 NIV).

Day 58

CALL THE DOCTOR

When my children were growing up, we had a family doctor that did not believe in making his patients wait forever before they got in to see him. I could drive to the next town, see the doctor, and be home while people in our town would still be sitting in the waiting room of a local physician. My appointment one morning was for 10:40 and by 11:15 I was on my way back home. I had an allergic reaction to the dust I breathed in while helping my husband clean out the garage, and it started a mess. I had acute pharyngitis, acute sinusitis, and otitis. Translated: a very sore throat, a very stuffy head, and an ear infection. I didn't think there was anything cute about any of them! (Please excuse the pun.) When a person is feeling so terrible, it is a blessing not to have to sit in the waiting room being miserable – even worth the extra drive time to get there. My doctor's policy made it a lot easier to deal with young children in the waiting room. They could be corralled better in an examination room.

I feel blessed that the Master Physician has no waiting room. He is available all the time with no appointment necessary. He never goes on vacation and is never tied up in a meeting. Even if someone else needs His attention at the same time I do, He can deal with it. Although it is hard for my finite mind to comprehend, God is always here wherever I am. I do not have to drive somewhere to get to His office. He knows my needs and fills them more than abundantly. What a joy it is to be a part of His family!

Sara Ray

"Bless the Lord, O my soul,
And all that is within me, bless His holy name.
Bless the Lord, O my soul,
And forget none of His benefits;
Who pardons all your iniquities,
Who heals all your diseases;
Who redeems your life from the pit,
Who crowns you with lovingkindness and compassion;
Who satisfies your years with good things,
So that your youth is renewed like the eagle" (Psalm 103:1-5 NASB).

Day 59

THINKING FOGGY

One Sunday morning I emerged from my bed while it was still dark. I kept track of the sunrise as I prepared for my trip to church, needing to be there at 7:30 a.m. for choir practice. As time drew closer for me to leave, I began to notice that the area just above the ground was becoming rather misty. By the time I pulled my minivan out of the garage, it was downright foggy.

As I drove along, there were some areas where all I could see was the road directly in front of me; the rest disappeared into the fog. It seemed quite eerie, yet I knew that the road kept going even though I was not able to see it. I would go through the dense mist for a while and then all of a sudden I would drive into an area where the sun was shining, and there was no evidence of the fog. After passing through the gloomy fog, the sunshine-brightened autumn leaves seemed more colorful than usual. However, it was not long before I would hit another foggy patch, and the road would seem like it had disappeared again.

There was one area that I assumed would be very foggy. It included a bridge over a large creek and a very narrow stretch of road that had no shoulder; the ground dropped off sharply on both sides. I hated to drive through it on nice days, let alone foggy ones. The alternate routes to avoid this area take me quite a bit out of my way in one direction or another, so I usually clench my teeth and drive through it.

Much to my surprise, that particular area was one of the sunny patches along my route. The fog did not appear again until I was well past it. (And yes, I thanked the Lord for that blessing!) As I drew closer to the church building, the fog became wisps here and there and then vanished altogether.

I began to think of how my drive to church resembled our trip through this life. We go through sunshine and shadow, darkness and light. Sometimes the way is clear in front of us and at other times all we can see is the small stretch of road that is right in front of us. If we look into the distance, there is nothing discernible. We go along for a while, trusting that the road is taking us where we need to go. Then the fog vanishes, and we burst into glorious light and enjoy a time of peace and contentment before we enter another patch of foggy weather. Places we expect to be gloomy may not be, and places we think there will be light may be dark as we travel through them.

One thing we know as we journey on: the way has been prepared, and as long as we stay on the right road, we have the assurance that we will make it to our final destination. We may not be able to see what lies ahead; however, there is one who does, and He can be depended on to be our eyes when we cannot rely on our own vision. If our focus is on Christ instead of on the fog around us, we can rest assured that He will see us through. And when we reach Heaven, there will not be any fog to keep us from seeing His blessed face!

"Make me know Your ways, O Lord;
Teach me Your paths.
Lead me in Your truth and teach me,
For You are the God of my salvation;
For You I wait all the day" (Psalm 25:4-5 NASB).

"For momentary, light affliction is producing for us an eternal weight of glory far beyond all comparison, while we look not at the things which are seen, but at the things which are not seen; for the things which are seen are temporal, but the things which are not seen are eternal" (2 Corinthians 4:17-18 NASB).

Day 60

THE OLD RED ROOSTER

After my marriage, I lived over three hundred miles away from my mother. The main way we kept in touch was by telephone. During one of our conversations, I was trying to describe to her a kitchen remodeling project that we had underway. She asked lots of questions and I answered them; however, there was a communication problem in the form of a red rooster.

Mom had had a rooster named Blaze for several years. His comb got frostbitten one winter, as did parts of the toes on one of his feet. They eventually just rotted off. Then the neighborhood dogs managed to catch Blaze and pull out his tail feathers. Mom decided that she should keep him in at night–in the house! She had a makeshift cage that she secured him in so that he didn't roam around freely, although there were times when she let him loose.

During the telephone conversation mentioned above, I would be in the middle of an explanation when I would hear Blaze crow loudly. "Could you please repeat that?" Mom would ask.

After several times of telling her the same thing, only to be interrupted by the rooster crowing again, I was more than frustrated. "Mom, for goodness' sake, put that rooster outside where he belongs!" I emphatically declared. She did so, and we were finally able to complete our telephone chat without interruption.

Following that conversation with my mother, I was convicted to write about what transpired. The Lord inspired me with the idea of how to use it in a devotion.

We often have things in our lives that interfere with what God is telling us. They may not belong where we have placed them, or we may have allowed them to remain once they found their way in. We don't hear His entire message for us due to loud interruptions from that which we shouldn't be hearing in the first place. Sometimes we listen so long to the wrong things that it becomes difficult to discern the right things. Caught up in what is going on around us, we lose sight of eternity. We focus on the here and now instead of the hereafter. God's voice becomes just another sound in the din around us. And we are made aware of the fact that we hear more from the noise around us than from the One we love most.

Along with the realization that we are missing out on the Lord's message comes the responsibility to rid ourselves of that which is interfering in our conversation with Him. And we should do so even when others do not understand why we are giving up something we enjoy doing. After all, it is the Lord's voice that matters most.

> "Now choose life, so that you and your children may live and that you may love the Lord your God, listen to his voice, and hold fast to him. For the Lord is your life" (Deuteronomy 30:19b-20a NIV).

> "But whatever things were gain to me, those things I have counted as loss for the sake of Christ. More than that, I count all things to be loss in view of the surpassing value of knowing Christ Jesus my Lord, for whom I have suffered the loss of all things, and count them but rubbish in order that I may gain Christ" (Philippians 3:7-8 NASB).

Day 61

DRY BONES

One of my very favorite stories in the Old Testament is the account of Ezekiel and the dry bones (Ezekiel 37:1-14). The Lord took Ezekiel and set him in a valley full of very dry bones. After leading the prophet back and forth among them, the Lord asked him an interesting question. "Son of man, can these bones live?" I love Ezekiel's answer: "O Sovereign Lord, you alone know."

As Ezekiel was looking around him, he could see no sign of life. All he saw was an enormous pile of sun-bleached bones. Common sense would have had him answer, "No!" to the Lord's question. But since Ezekiel was an intimate friend of the Creator of the Universe, he was quick to realize that only that Creator knew the answer to His own question. Ezekiel was aware that God could use His power to restore life to dry bones if He chose to do so. However, Ezekiel did not presume that God would do so by replying, "Yes, they can live." He left the answer in the hands of the Lord.

God then told Ezekiel to prophesy to the bones. Can you imagine being a preacher and having your congregation made up of nothing but old dried up skeletal remains? (Although some churches seem so dead, maybe it is possible …) Ezekiel did as he was commanded, and a miraculous thing began to happen. The bones came together, and tendons, flesh, and skin appeared on them. Even though they now were bodies instead of just bones, they were still dead. God spoke to Ezekiel again and told him to prophesy so that breath would come from the four winds and breathe into the bodies so that they

129

would live. Ezekiel obeyed; the bodies came to life and stood on their feet, and there was a vast army.

Have you ever gone through times in your life when you feel all dried up? It seems like it is all you can do to keep on going. And you wonder why in the world you feel that way. After all, you are a child of God. You know deep down inside that you can trust Him. But everything seems so useless. God is there, but you can't grasp His nearness. Your prayers seem to bounce off the ceiling. You don't want to bother anyone else with your discontent; besides, it is not something you can explain, anyway. You may withdraw into your own little world, or you might keep plodding along, hoping that your dry spell will end. Somehow, the joy of living has departed from your everyday existence. If you have not been there, then trust me when I tell you that there are days (and weeks and months) like that. I have been there.

God can take the dried out days and turn them into something alive and vibrant. He restores the joy of living and fleshes out our purpose in life once again. It is not fun to go through the dry spells, but they can give us a perspective that we would not gain any other way. We can use what we have been through to help others weather their own dry spells. Sometimes the help comes from the knowledge that other people go through desert times as well. Even those folk that we consider to be spiritual giants have had times of drought in their lives.

If you feel like you are dry bones in Ezekiel's valley, just think of this. God has wonderful things in store for you. He alone knows all the answers. In His perfect time, He will breathe new joy into your life, bring you back to your feet, and get you headed in the proper direction once again.

> "Then he said to me: "Son of man, these bones are the people of Israel. They say, 'Our bones are dried up and our hope is gone; we are cut off.' Therefore prophesy and say to them: 'This is what the Sovereign Lord says: My people, I am going to open your graves and bring you up from them; I will bring you back to the land of Israel. Then you, my people, will know that I am the Lord, when I open your graves and bring you up from them. I will put my Spirit in you and you will live, and I will settle you in your own land. Then you will know that I the Lord have spoken, and I have done it, declares the Lord'" (Ezekiel 37:11-14 NIV).

Day 62

BLACKBERRIES AND HORNETS

One of my dad's favorite pastimes in July was to go blackberry picking. He was an expert at finding the best berries, and his containers rarely had any of the sticks and leaves, etc. that are usually found in a berry bucket. He could pick two gallons of berries before anyone else had gotten their bucket even half full. My mom would freeze the berries that we did not use at once. She placed them on cookie sheets until they were frozen, and then placed them in plastic bags. That way they did not all stick together in a huge clump. There was a downfall to Mom's method of preservation. Her children, including me, discovered that they were really good if you put some of the frozen berries in a bowl, sprinkled them with sugar, and poured a little milk over them. The milk would freeze around the berries, and it made quite a tasty treat! I wonder why Mom never seemed to have frozen enough berries for very many cobblers during the winter ...

Dad knew a lot about nature, and he loved to pass the information to his children. Something that he always told us was not to run from a hornet or yellow jacket because they feel threatened by moving objects. He taught us to never, ever swat at one. Dad's solution was to stand very still until the insect went away. He emphasized to us that this was very important if we were near a nest. Then we were to creep slowly away, so as not to attract the attention of the stinging insects.

Now I am going to tie the two seemingly unrelated paragraphs together. One day when I went blackberry picking with my sisters I was in a different area than they were. We could hear each other, but we could not see each other. My dad had taught us that you could get more berries if you stayed put and picked the small ones as well as the huge ones. Only after all the ripe ones within reach were picked should you move on. I was picking away and all of a sudden I felt a sharp pain on the top of my foot. I looked down only to see some hornets, stinging away! Unlike honeybees, hornets can sting multiple times because they do not lose their stingers. After looking even more closely, I spied a hornet's nest – right in front of my foot.

Because of years of training by my dad, I knew not to run. If I did, I would have a whole nest of hornets after me instead of the few that were already expressing their anger. I began to inch slowly away, creeping along until I got several feet away from that nest. Then I took off running for home, needing to tend to my poor foot, which was quite swollen by the time I got there.

My natural tendency was to run from those hornets as fast as I could. But because I listened and learned from my father, I chose to take a smarter course of action. Even though it seemed like I would never get away from that hornets' nest, I chose to go with what I had learned instead of my natural reaction. In the same way, we need to listen and learn from our heavenly Father. He has given us instructions that often go against our human natures, but it will be much better for us in the end if we choose to obey them instead of following our human tendencies. It may even seem painful at the time to do so, but the pain is a lot less than what we would go through if we choose to disobey.

It is important to know our Father's instructions so that when we are faced with a situation we will know how to react. If my dad had not taught me to get slowly away from hornets, I would have taken off running, which would have been the wrong thing to do. We have a very wise heavenly Father, and it makes all the difference in the world when we follow His leading in our lives.

> "For the grace of God has appeared that offers salvation to all people.
> It teaches us to say 'No' to ungodliness and worldly passions, and to
> live self-controlled, upright and godly lives in this present age, while

we wait for the blessed hope – the appearing of the glory of our great God and Savior, Jesus Christ, who gave himself for us to redeem us from all wickedness and to purify for himself a people that are his very own, eager to do what is good" (Titus 2:11-14 NIV).

Day 63

WATCH OUT FOR THE POUNCE!

Something happened one afternoon that I found quite distressing. I was sitting on the couch in the living room reading a magazine. All of a sudden there was a loud THUD! It startled my cat Tennyson, who was sitting in front of the picture window. He jumped up like he had been shot. I went over to look out the window. There was a little bird lying between a bush and the house; it was alive but in shock. Knowing that the cats outside would find it, I decided to go out and pick the bird up and put it where they would not bother it.

Bright, beady eyes watched me as I leaned down to pick up the feathered victim. The little bird seemed to understand that I wanted to help it. I had put on gloves before I touched it, and it seemed content to lie in the palm of my hand while it regained its bearings. When it began to move around a bit, I decided that I would take it to the backyard bird feeder, where I knew that the cats could not reach it. By the time I reached the feeder, the bird had perked up quite a bit, and it sat perched on my index finger. Just as I stretched out my hand towards the feeder, the bird decided that it was time to fly away. However, it still did not have its full faculties, so all it could do was flutter to the ground.

As soon as the bird hit the ground– POUNCE! Our outdoor cat Missy grabbed the poor thing in her mouth and ran away with it as fast as she could go. I tried to catch her, but she was too quick for me. She managed to elude my grasp, and I finally quit chasing her, knowing that I was fighting a losing battle. I saw her go under a bush, carrying her birdie lunch. I yelled across the yard at her, "You make my heart hurt!" Of course, Missy didn't care. She just enjoyed her snack.

Can't you just picture the Lord holding us as we are stunned and bruised from life? He lifts us up with gentle hands and holds us close, warming us with His wonderful love. We bask in the sunshine of His presence, relaxed and trusting in His care. What a feeling! Ah, but that is not the end of the story ...

At some point we decide that we are ready to fly again; we can do it on our own, thank you, please. And so we flutter away from the shelter of God's care – deliberately stepping out of His protection. Guess what? Our enemy is ready and waiting to POUNCE! Before we know it, the old devil has us in his clutches. Like the frightened bird, we are afraid that this is it – the end of the road. But we cry out to our Father in Heaven because we still have one thing left: hope. And God hears us.

I might not have been able to get the bird away from Missy, but how thankful I am that our powerful Lord can rescue us from Satan's grasp. He does it again and again and again. Like when I worry over things that have not happened. When I fret about things I have no control over. Even when I put my will above His will for me. As He holds me close, I determine never to go out of His protection again. I wish I could say that I would never do so, but I know better than to tell that whopper! All I can truthfully say is that I am on a journey along with you; a journey towards a place where we will be in the presence of God forever. And He will help us get to that place where Satan will never pounce again.

> "Be of sober spirit, be on the alert. Your adversary, the devil, prowls around like a roaring lion, seeking someone to devour. But resist him, firm in your faith, knowing that the same experiences of suffering are being accomplished by your brethren who are in the world. After you have suffered for a little while, the God of all grace, who called you to His eternal glory in Christ, will Himself perfect, confirm, strengthen and establish you. To Him be dominion forever and ever. Amen" (1 Peter 5:8-11 NASB).

Day 64

LET GO OF THE THROTTLE!

One of the things we invested in when we moved to the country was a little tiller. It only weighed twenty pounds, but boy could it dig! I was able to handle it all by myself, which was a good thing. Or so it seemed when we bought it. Then I decided to put the tiller to use and enlarge an area that my husband Bob had tilled previously. There was a rose bush planted in it, and I wanted to plant two more. It seemed like an ideal location since they were climbing roses, and it was right beside a fence. I took the tiller out of the barn and carried it to the spot where I wanted to dig. I managed to get it started with no problem.

The tiller and I got along fine until it hit a rock. When that happened, the tiller began to bounce until it got away from the rock. Fortunately, I had used it before, and I knew to keep a tight grip on it at all times. I never knew when I was going to encounter a rock or root or some other obstacle.

I had to stop several times and pick up rocks, digging them out with a shovel if they were very big. Then I could continue tilling. After dealing with several rocks, for some reason I let my guard down. I was standing facing the fence and letting the tiller do its thing full speed ahead. All of a sudden, it began to bounce. And they were not just small bounces, but the tiller was leaping pretty far up into the air.

It was at that point when the tines of the tiller got caught in the fence, and it began to climb its way up! I wondered what in the world I was going to do. Here I was, standing out in the yard with my tiller making great strides at going over the top of the fence. Suddenly, I had one of those, "Well, DUH!" moments. I let go of the gas lever, and the tiller quit climbing! Then all I had to do was lift it off the fence, dig out the rock, and get on with my project.

It seems like we are constantly going at life at full throttle. We want to zoom over obstacles as if they are not there. Sometimes we think that if we ignore them, they will go away. At other times, we keep worrying about them, wishing they would disappear. However, we do not want to slow down and remove them. Our goal is to get as much done as possible in the time that God has granted us. While that may not be bad in and of itself, we forget to take the time to enjoy what God has given us. Worst of all, we forget to acknowledge God's presence in our lives. And sometimes God gives us a "Well, DUH!" moment.

"I am here!" He seems to say. "Let go of your busyness and enjoy My presence. Get in tune with Me and I will remove the obstacles. Make Me the focus of your life and I will keep you going."

Maybe you need to take some time today– and every day–to enjoy God in your life. Ease off the throttle and give Him control. Let Him fill you with a wonderful sense of His presence. You will be renewed and refreshed and get more accomplished than if you keep going full speed ahead. And when the obstacles come, as they always do, you will be better prepared to deal with them.

"Cease striving and know that I am God;
I will be exalted among the nations, I will be
exalted in the earth" (Psalm 46:10 NASB).

"O Lord, my heart is not proud, nor my eyes haughty;
Nor do I involve myself in great matters,
Or in things too difficult for me.
Surely I have composed and quieted my soul;
Like a weaned child rests against his mother,
My soul is like a weaned child within me" (Psalm 131:1-2 NASB).

Day 65

FROM HAS-BEENS TO HAS BEANS

For some reason, I never feel that I have had a successful year of canning and preserving food unless I have put up plenty of green beans. My goal used to be at least fifty-two quarts of beans; I arrived at this number by figuring a quart of beans per week for one year.

It was the first year my family moved to the country after living in town for over twenty years. I was excited about having a garden and not being required to purchase green beans for canning purposes. When our green beans began to be ready to pick, I was quite disappointed. Out of two and one-half rows of beans, I barely managed to get one canner load (seven quarts), plus enough to cook for a meal. The second picking only yielded two more canner loads. By then, the bean plants were looking pitiful. They had stopped blooming, and the beans were all but gone off of them. My husband had planted another row of beans a few weeks after the first ones, and I was hoping that they would do much better. We decided to pull up the old plants and plant something else in their place, some type of fall crop. Being in no hurry, we left them alone until we were ready to mess with them. Thank goodness we did.

It wasn't long before I began to notice that the older bean plants were blooming again. They produced and produced and produced beans. I canned beans for us, beans for my in-laws, taught a friend how to can beans, and gave lots of beans away. And there were still beans. I finally started leaving them on the vines because I had other produce to deal with, and I got tired of picking them. Those plants did not want to give up – they still had beans on them when we mowed the garden after the first hard frost.

Have you ever had someone in your life that you have prayed for and helped and worried about and wondered if they would ever get their life in order? Just when it seems they have gotten straightened out they start all over again into the same old routines you thought they had managed to get over. It seems like the cycle is never-ending, and you come to the point where you want just to give up.

You begin to feel that you have expended all the effort you are going to put out for that person. They ask for advice but don't heed it. They want help but are not willing to put forth any effort on their own. It is not that you don't care about them anymore, you are just worn out from the way they break your heart over and over when they fall back into their old pattern of living. There are two words that describe how you feel about their treatment of you: "used" and "abused". And so you decide to give up on them. "Lord, they are in Your hands now because I can't help them anymore!" you pray. Actually, it is in His hands where they needed to be placed all along.

Although you feel all but sure there is no hope for someone, the Lord has a way of bringing new life out of a dying plant. And the fruit they bear can be phenomenal because others see the change God has wrought in them. God has a way of placing hope back into situations we consider hopeless and using those situations to further His Kingdom. The prayers we keep praying for those we have given up on CAN make a difference in a lost and dying world.

"Therefore confess your sins to each other and pray for each other so that you may be healed. The prayer of a righteous person is powerful and effective. … My brothers and sisters, if one of you should wander from the truth and someone should bring that person back, remember this: Whoever turns a sinner from the error of their ways will save him from death and cover over a multitude of sins" (James 5:16, 19-20 NIV).

"For the eyes of the Lord are toward the righteous,
And His ears attend to their prayer,
But the face of the Lord is against those
who do evil" (1 Peter 3:12 NASB).

Day 66

AND YOUR NAME IS ...

I have always been intrigued by the story of how my late husband managed to have the last name of Ray. The surprise came two generations before him. When Bob's paternal grandfather decided to get married, his mother knew that she had to inform him that his last name was not the one he had been using, it was "Ray." It seems that she had only been married to his father for a very short time; they had divorced before Granddad was old enough to know his father. She later remarried a man with a different last name and raised Granddad by that surname. However, for him to obtain a marriage license, he had to know his legal last name. As I recounted this story to a friend, we discussed how surprised his wife-to-be must have been. You know how girls like to practice writing their future names as they dream about being "Mrs. Hubby". All of a sudden she would have had to doodle "Mrs. Ray" instead of "Mrs. Otherwise"!

Can you imagine the impact it would have on your life to suddenly find out that you were not who you thought you were? Your whole sense of identity would be changed. In this day and age, you would probably have to go through all kinds of therapy to "find yourself". Thankfully, Grandma and Granddad Ray went on about life; their marriage of over fifty years produced four sons, one of which was my father-in-law.

Granddad was not entitled to the last name of the man who raised him because he was never legally adopted. When we accept Christ, however, we do become adopted into God's family. We are legal heirs of all God has in store for us. We will not come to judgment day and hear the Lord say, "Depart from me – I do not know you!" because our relationship with Christ gives us an inheritance of eternal life. Our identity has been changed from "Condemned" to "Redeemed". What a joy it is to know that we are a part of an eternal family whose Father loved us enough to make us His own through the sacrifice of His firstborn Son!

> "Praise be to the God and Father of our Lord Jesus Christ, who has blessed us in the heavenly realms with every spiritual blessing in Christ. For he chose us in him before the creation of the world to be holy and blameless in his sight. In love he predestined us for adoption to sonship through Jesus Christ, in accordance with his pleasure and will – to the praise of his glorious grace, which he has freely given us in the One he loves" (Ephesians 1:3-6 NIV).

> "For you have not received a spirit of slavery leading to fear again, but you have received a spirit of adoption as sons by which we cry out, 'Abba! Father!' The Spirit Himself testifies with our spirit that we are children of God, and if children, heirs also, heirs of God and fellow heirs with Christ, if indeed we suffer with Him so that we may also be glorified with Him. ... And not only this, but also we ourselves, having the first fruits of the Spirit, even we ourselves groan within ourselves, waiting eagerly for our adoption as sons, the redemption of our body" (Romans 8:15-17, 23 NASB).

Day 67

BUILDING UP FOR THE BIG EVENT

Have you ever spent a lot of time, effort, and energy getting ready for a big event? Perhaps it was a wedding or graduation. Maybe it was an anniversary celebration or a retirement party. Whatever it happened to be, there comes a time when it is over. Done. Completed. It might not have met your expectations, it could have, or it possibly may have exceeded them. No matter the outcome, now your big event is in the past.

As I reflect back over my life, I remember all the preparation work for so many things I have done through the years. I think of the hours spent getting crafts ready for Vacation Bible School. The days I spent sewing for various weddings. The effort spent shopping for just the right items to create just the right effect for a certain special occasion. Time spent in my kitchen cooking and baking to provide homemade treats. And if my home were to be used as the location, there would also be cleaning and dusting and other household tasks added to the list of things to accomplish before the event took place.

Every one of those things I worked so hard for has one thing in common: they are finished. There are no do-overs. I may choose to be involved in something similar, but the new event will stand on its own and not be a repeat of a prior happening.

No matter the success (or not) of something into which I have placed a lot of time and energy, when it is over I usually feel a big letdown. Sometimes it is also accompanied by a sense of satisfaction over a job well done; however, everything I accomplished for that particular purpose is now nothing but a memory, be it good or not-so-good. And I have to admit that there have been times that I wondered if all my efforts made any difference after all. Did the time I spent have meaning? Did my hard work pay off or was it just fruitless labor for the sake of appearances? Could I have done more? Should I have done less? Is there a lesson for me here?

The sense of letdown after something we have looked forward to for a long time is not uncommon. The hoopla has passed, and everyday life resumes once more. Another event comes along, and we pour effort into it. When it is over, we experience that letdown feeling again, and then the cycle starts over.

> You know, my friends, there will come a day when our life event is over. Finished. Completed. We cannot go back and re-live it. But if we know Jesus, and He is our Savior and Lord, we will not experience a letdown. We will hear Him say, "Well done, good and faithful servant!" (Matthew 25:21 NIV). The afterward is Heaven, as described in 1 Corinthians 2:9 NCV:

> "But as it is written in the Scriptures:
> 'No one has ever seen this,
> and no one has ever heard about it.
> No one has ever imagined
> what God has prepared for those who love him.'"

I don't know about you, but I look forward to the time when the "Big Event" is never over, and we live it forever!

> "And I heard a loud voice from the throne, saying, 'Now God's presence is with people, and he will live with them, and they will be his people. God himself will be with them and will be their God. He will wipe away every tear from their eyes, and there will be no more death, sadness, crying, or pain, because all the old ways are gone.'

> The One who was sitting on the throne said, 'Look! I am making everything new!' Then he said, 'Write this, because these words are true and can be trusted.'

The One on the throne said to me, 'It is finished. I am the Alpha and the Omega, the Beginning and the End. I will give free water from the spring of the water of life to anyone who is thirsty. Those who win the victory will receive this, and I will be their God, and they will be my children'" (Revelation 21:3-7 NCV).

Day 68

JUST HANGIN' AROUND

I am going to tell you about the day that we hanged my brother. (If "hanged" seems like an awkward word, tell my high school English teacher. She drilled into us, "Pictures are hung; people are hanged.") Before you panic, let me reassure you on two counts:

> We did not hang him by the neck.
> John is still alive.

My brother John is the youngest of six children. I am the oldest; there is a nine-and-one-half year difference between us. When I was somewhere around twelve or thirteen years old, my parents decided that I was old enough to babysit. They would always have a neighbor on stand-by in case I needed help. One particular Saturday morning, Mom and Dad needed to go somewhere, so they left me in charge of all my siblings, including John.

John was a handful all by himself. My mother could tell you about the day that she followed him around cleaning up after the disasters he created. He turned on the water in the bathtub and then went out of the bathroom, locking the door behind him. He dumped a whole box of detergent into the washer and then turned on the washer. While Mom was cleaning up one mess, he was off into something else, and so her whole day went. John was not being naughty on purpose; he was just busy. Needless to say, my sisters and I were not too thrilled about being responsible for him. We had things we wanted to do and to keep a close eye on John was not one of them.

I don't remember which one of us came up with the Idea, but it seemed brilliant at the time. We would make sure that John could not get into trouble by fastening him to a rope where he could only reach so far. He still managed to find something to get into. That was when the thought hit us: if John's feet could not touch the ground, then John could not manage to get into trouble. We fastened a rope to the ceiling at a place where the plaster was off, allowing us to loop it around the joist. Then we tied the rope around John. We even put pads under his armpits so that the rope would not cut into him. We pulled him off the floor just high enough so that his feet could not touch it. He also could not reach the knots in the rope and untie himself because they were behind him. John stayed out of trouble!

Trouble came looking for us, however, when my mother got home and found her youngest child dangling from the living room ceiling. She was extremely upset. She never even listened to the, "But Mom ... we didn't hurt him. And he didn't get into trouble this way." I can't remember what our punishment was, and I am not so sure that it is anything I want to remember! Suffice it to say, we never tried anything like that again.

How often in our lives do we try to handle our problems in an inappropriate manner? We try to find an easy way out instead of dealing with trouble head-on. Many times we end up in a more difficult situation that what we faced in the first place. The sad thing is that we never seem to learn from our mistakes; we still keep looking for an easy fix, no matter how temporary it is. And God waits for us to ask Him for help. He has had the right remedy all along. It may seem harder in the first place, but think of all the pain that we avoid in the end. (I am somehow confident that after hanging John, there was much pain in the end– the rear end– for my sisters and me!) God has the solution for all the problems we face. When we know what He wants us to do, we need to do it even if it means choosing a harder path instead of trying to find an easy way out. Believe it or not, the harder path will end up being the easiest path in the long run because we can rely on God's strength to keep us on it.

"If you hide your sins, you will not succeed.
If you confess and reject them, you will receive
mercy" (Proverbs 28:13 NCV).

"Be humble under God's powerful hand so he will lift you up when
the right time comes. Give all your worries to him, because he cares
about you" (1 Peter 5:6-7 NCV).

Day 69

MENDING

The past several years, I have been a lot better about keeping my mending pile to a minimum. This phenomenon happened because one of my children came to me with something that needed to be repaired. When I told him to put it in the mending pile, the remark was made, "Well, that is the last time I will ever see that!" I looked through the pile and realized that my children had outgrown a lot of the things that were stacking up there. I got busy and completed all of the projects that were in the pile, and I have not let it get very big since then. Some of the things were given away, and some were passed down to a younger sibling. I discarded others because they were not worth fixing. My children were happy to have use of their clothes again, and my husband was pleased to have some of his favorites back in commission.

Each of our lives has a mending pile of relationships that need repairs. Some are major sewing jobs while some just need darning. The size of the pile depends on how well we keep up with what we need to do to keep our relationships in good working order. There are times that the problem may lie with the other person, just like most of the things in my mending pile did not belong to me. However, I was the one who could fix them. Sometimes we can be the mender that helps people restore their relationships with others. Or we can be the one to reach out and darn a damaged friendship, even though it was the other person who caused the problem in the first place.

The most important relationship we have is the one with our Heavenly Father. If the seams in it are loose or ripped out, we can be guaranteed that we caused the problem because God loves us and does His very best to keep the relationship healthy. If we get holes in the knees of our pants because we have stumbled and fallen, He will patch the holes. If we begin to fray at the edges, He binds us with His loving care. If the buttons pop off, the zipper breaks, or the snaps lose their grip, He can make them right if we surrender them to His healing touch. God's mending pile does not build up because He is always ready to fix whatever needs repaired. All we have to do is ask and then trust that He will do as He promised.

"Everyone who believes that Jesus is the Christ is born of God, and everyone who loves the father loves his child as well. This is how we know that we love the children of God: by loving God and carrying out his commands. In fact, this is love for God: to keep his commands. And his commands are not burdensome, for everyone born of God overcomes the world. This is the victory that has overcome the world, even our faith" (1 John 5:1-4 NIV).

Day 70

LAUGHTER

I have read in several different places about the healing power of laughter. Laughter is also good for disease prevention. If we can take ourselves a lot less seriously and learn to laugh at our mistakes, we can lessen a lot of the effects of stress in our lives. God gave us laughter for a reason. So I am going to tell a story today about me. And I hope you laugh!

Several years ago, my youngest sister informed me that two teaspoons of cider vinegar mixed with eight ounces of water would help people lose weight. The concoction was to be sipped as they were eating their meals. My thoughts on this information were:

> I would not be using drugs or going on a weird diet.
> It is relatively inexpensive.
> There is vitamin C in the vinegar.
> What can it hurt to try it?

And so I did. Try it, that is. Sure enough, it really did help. My clothes began fitting a little looser after only a week. Then my husband Bob decided to try it as well. He was able to tighten his belt two notches after a while. Some people thought we were nuts to drink vinegar water, but hey! It was working!

Then came the day that Bob was not going to come home for lunch as he normally did. I decided to fix beets for lunch because I like them, and Bob can't stand them. My son Jonathan would eat beets, but I can't remember how Adam or Molly felt about them, which tells you I didn't prepare them very often.

On this particular day, the humor at our lunch table was quite evident. There were times that Molly would start rattling on and on about one subject or another. Jonathan and I would try not to laugh at her. We could not even look at each other, or we would lose control. I think this might have been one of those days. But something had us on the brink of a good laugh.

Just as I took my last big swig of vinegar water, I happened to glance at Jonathan. He grinned at me. Because he had been eating beets, his teeth were fuchsia pink. That did it. I gave a loud snort and tried to swallow what was in my mouth, but it wouldn't go down because I was laughing too hard. So it came out my nose instead.

Now I don't know if you have ever had vinegar in your nose, but take my advice and DO NOT try it. It burns like crazy. Here I was, supposed to be the adult and the shining example for my children, choking and snuffling and laughing all at the same time. My offspring were about to split a gut watching their mother's dilemma. After this incident, the vinegar water at meals died a sudden death. And I have the inches to prove it!

I am not going to try to make a parallel between this story and our lives. I just wanted you to have a good laugh. On me. And don't take yourself or life so seriously! God gave us laughter and blessed us with abundant joy!

> "He will yet fill your mouth with laughter
> and your lips with shouts of joy" (Job 8:21 NIV).

Day 71

SHARPENED TO THE POINT

Over the course of the years, my family learned this: DO NOT use Mom's sewing scissors for anything other than fabric!!!!!! That command includes paper, pipe cleaners, plastic, hair, and anything else they could think of. If it is not fabric, do not– let me repeat– DO NOT use Mom's sewing scissors to cut it. It is worse than annoying to get everything ready to cut out a garment, have the pattern laid out and pinned to the fabric, only to begin cutting and have the scissors chew the fabric instead of slicing right through it. Or to have them cut smoothly until you get to the tip of the blades and then twist the fabric instead of snipping it.

I also hate it when the smaller pair of scissors kept beside my sewing machine mangles the thread I am trying to cut instead of clipping it. If you have ever tried to thread a needle with mangled thread, you will understand. Someone in my family was known to trim his mustache with my small scissors, which tended to loosen them as well as dull the blades. I couldn't figure out what was going on with them until I finally caught the culprit in action.

We who are Christians are called to be different. We are set apart for a purpose, much like my sewing scissors. We are to remain sharp and ready to be used by God for the furthering of His kingdom. It is very frustrating to me to find my scissors lacking the sharpness I expect to find when I begin cutting fabric. Can you imagine how the Lord feels when He wants to use us for His purposes only to find that we have been dulled by using our minds and bodies in worldly pursuits? We get so caught up in the here and now that we forget to keep ourselves sharpened and ready for the Master's use. We tolerate the sin that we are supposed to avoid – even to the point of becoming caught up in it.

Scissors can be sharpened; our hearts and minds can be sharpened as well. With the whetstone of God's Word and the polishing of prayer, we can get rid of the dullness that hinders our use in the Kingdom of God.

"O God, it is You who knows my folly,
And my wrongs are not hidden from You.
May those who wait for You not be ashamed
through me, O Lord God of hosts;
May those who seek You not be dishonored through
me, O God of Israel" (Psalm 69:5-6 NASB).

"Retain the standard of sound words which you have heard from me, in the faith and love which are in Christ Jesus. Guard, through the Holy Spirit who dwells in us, the treasure which has been entrusted to you" (2 Timothy 1:13-14 NASB).

Day 72

GOOD NUTRITION

A friend of mine brought me a baby kitten that was two days old. The kitten's mother had rejected her, and I became her substitute mom. When she had reached the age where it was time to wean her from her bottle I began trying to get her to eat solid food. At first, she would sniff the cat food but had no idea of what to do with it. So I scrounged up a baby spoon I had kept from when my children were small and fed her little bits at a time. She did not want to open her mouth and bite; she wanted to suck at everything. As long as I pried her mouth open and put the food in it, she would eat.

Then we progressed to the stage where the kitten smelled the food and wanted it, but she refused to eat on her own. She would not even lick it off the spoon. We ended up with smelly canned cat food all over me, all over her, and some on the floor. Neither one of us was a very happy camper. The kitten really howled when I gave her a bath, and I did my share of grumbling as I changed clothes.

Finally, the kitten began doing much better. She would still start out sucking at the food, but she began to realize that she needed to open her jaws and bite it and then chew it up. Then I had to try and get her to stop kneading her food as she was eating it ...

Many people want to study Scripture only if someone else feeds it to them. They have no desire to make an effort to feed themselves. What they fail to

154

realize is that they may not be getting the nourishment that they need to grow. They are only getting what someone else decides to give them, and it is highly possible that it does not meet their nutritional needs.

Others seem hungry for God's Word, but they are afraid to study it because they don't think they can understand it by themselves. They seem to think there is some hidden meaning behind most Scripture that only theologians can discover. They are very reluctant to open a Bible and dig in.

Then there are those people who see the Word of God as something to be enjoyed. They might have questions as they study, but they realize that it is okay to ask the Lord for wisdom to understand, and that is also okay to ask fellow Christians for their insight on the matter. They come to know that prayer and Bible study go hand in hand. And God meets their nutritional needs by the power of His Spirit that is at work in their lives.

Which type of eater are you?

"Do your best to present yourself to God as one approved, a worker who does not need to be ashamed and who correctly handles the word of truth" (2 Timothy 2:15 NIV).

Day 73

NEVER LOSE POWER

It seems like the human race is always looking for a power source. If we can't do something one way, we will try something else. There are many, many research projects that are seeking to find alternate sources of fuel so that we will not be so dependent on petroleum. People are afraid that the fossil-fuel sources will be depleted. Several ways have been found to use power from the sun. Water power has been harnessed to create electric power. Coal-burning plants that produce electricity cause our air to be polluted. Then there is nuclear power. Although it creates energy, the waste products are dangerous.

No matter which way we turn, there appears to be no totally dependable source of power. Gasoline prices are often terrible. Alternative fuel looks like a better idea all the time. But so far, there is not an economical replacement for gas – at least for common, everyday people. Solar power relies on the presence of the sun. Several cloudy days in a row can severely hamper things that rely on solar energy. I have read in the newspaper that when droughts are expected during peak summer usage there may not be enough electricity to run all the air conditioners and other things that keep us all cool. Part of this is because there will not be as much water power to harness. Environmental concerns have all but nixed the usage of nuclear power. What mankind seeks is an unfailing, never-ending source of power.

Let's think about this. Unfailing: God. Never-ending: God. Source of power: God. Hmmm ...

I love the song "The Blood Will Never Lose Its Power" by Andraé Crouch. It fills my being with awe and worship. Of all the power sources we have available, there is one that never changes, never depletes, and never falters. If we have the blood of Jesus applied to our lives, there will be no power outage. His grace does not end; clouds do not block His love; no dangerous waste products result from the power that comes from the blood of Christ. Once we receive it, God never removes the Source of power from us. We can disconnect ourselves – after all, He has given us free will. However, once we have experienced His mighty power in our lives, we would be less than intelligent to deny ourselves the infinite source of energy that Christ has to offer. His blood will NEVER lose its power!

Scripture:

> "Great is our Lord and mighty in power;
> his understanding has no limit" (Psalm 147:5 NIV).

> "Now I know that the Lord saves his anointed;
> He will answer him from His holy heaven
> with the saving strength of His right hand" (Psalm 20:6 NASB).

> "The Son is the radiance of God's glory and the exact representation of his being, sustaining all things by his powerful word. After he had provided purification for sins, he sat down at the right hand of the Majesty in heaven" (Hebrews 1:3 NIV).

Day 74

CAN YOU HEAR HIS STILL, SMALL VOICE?

After the prophet Elijah had showed God's power on Mount Carmel by calling down fire from Heaven, his life was threatened by Queen Jezebel. Elijah became afraid and ran from her. He went into the desert, sat under a broom tree, and prayed that the Lord would take his life. Then he lay down and went to sleep. He was awakened by an angel, who told him to get up and eat. He found a cake of bread and a jar of water that had been placed beside his head. After eating and drinking, Elijah went back to sleep. He was awakened by the angel a second time to eat and drink. When he had finished doing so, Elijah traveled 40 days and 40 nights until he reached Mount Horeb, the mountain of God. He went into a cave and spent the night.

The Lord spoke to Elijah, saying, "What are you doing here, Elijah?"

Elijah began to complain bitterly. "I have done the work of God Almighty. The Israelites have not obeyed your laws; they have torn down your altars, they have killed all the prophets and I am the only one left. Now they are trying to kill me, too."

The Lord told Elijah, "Go out and stand on the mountain in the presence of the Lord, for the Lord is about to pass by."

A powerful wind blew through the mountains and broke rocks – but the Lord was not in the wind. Then an earthquake shook the mountain – but the Lord was not in the earthquake. Next, a raging fire swept by Elijah; however the Lord was not in the fire.

After the fire had passed, Elijah heard a gentle whisper – it was the Lord. When the Lord spoke to Elijah again, He assured Elijah that he would be taken care of, and informed him that there were 7000 others that had not left the one true God for false gods.

(This account of Elijah is found in 1 Kings 18 – 19)

Have you ever felt like Elijah? Sometimes, we are trying our best to do what God would have us do. Then when we see others, especially those that call themselves Christians, ignoring God's laws and "doing their own thing", we can get discouraged. It seems like our obedience is for nothing; we even get laughed at, ignored, and persecuted while "everyone else" is having a good time. We forget that there are others occupying the same boat we find ourselves in; others that are trying just as hard as we are to do what is right. Like Elijah, we begin to pity ourselves, and we grumble and complain about how hard it is to do God's will. We want to give up. It's not that we give up on God, but we forget that He is in control. We forget that without the Lord, we are nothing. We lose the closeness of His presence because we are too busy feeling sorry for ourselves to listen to His still, small voice.

The Lord showed Himself to Elijah, but not in the wind, the earthquake, nor the fire. He showed Himself in the gentle whisper. God reminded Elijah that He does not always choose the most obvious ways to work; many times the small things we ignore are God's way of working behind the scenes. If we are trusting Him and letting Him lead us, then we have little or no time for self-pity. When we allow God to work in our lives during the times we are the most discouraged, we are able to accomplish His good and perfect will for our lives.

"And we know that God causes all things to work together for good to those who love God, to those who are called according to His purpose" (Romans 8:28 NASB).

"Therefore, those also who suffer according to the will of God shall entrust their souls to a faithful Creator in doing what is right" (1 Peter 4:19 NASB).

Day 75

GIVE US THIS DAY

"Give us this day our daily bread." These words from what we know as 'The Lord's Prayer" are familiar to most of us, although those from younger generations may know them from a different translation.

I was trying to focus on prayer time one morning and decided to use the Lord's Prayer to keep my mind from roaming. I praised God for all that He is and all that He does. (Hallowed be Thy name.) I prayed for those of us in His church to be what we should be, and for His will to be done here on earth. Then I came to the part about the bread.

As I pondered the phrase, I thought about what the words "daily bread" could encompass. No, I am not some great spiritual giant who knows Greek and Hebrew and all that they convey with different words and verb forms that do not have a direct translation into the English language. I only can explain what I was sensing at the time of my communication with God.

Maybe "daily bread" could be thought of as "daily needs." What are my daily needs? My spiritual needs are as important as my physical needs. I need the Lord's strength to make it through each day. I need His wisdom for the things I am facing in the here and now. I require His guidance to make my paths straight and to keep my vision clear for the present. I am not in the past; therefore, I do not need "daily bread" for the past. I am not in the future; I do not need an overload of provisions for the future because they would overwhelm today. Bread that is good today might well be moldy tomorrow. My dependence on God for all my needs has to be for the time I am living right now. I know that I will always be living in the right now as opposed to the past (what has been) or the future (what will be).

"Forgive us our debts as we also have forgiven our debtors." That phrase is a sermon in itself! My Bible has a footnote stating that the debts are "sins of omission and commission" and that if we have forgiven "our debtors," we have *cancelled* that debt. In other words, we trust that when God forgives our sin, He will cancel it out. After all, Jesus died for us in order to make that possible. Not only did He die for us, but He died to self. The same is required for us when we are faced with the debts of others.

What if God truly forgave us the way we forgive others? I am afraid that I would live in trepidation because I know how something can trigger a memory, and I get upset over circumstances that happened in the past. I cannot change it, the other person(s) involved cannot change it; the situation is over, and there is no possibility of altering it. Maybe this is where the "daily bread" comes into play– I need the strength to refocus and see the other person(s) in the now and deal with them in today and not yesterday. I have to view them through God's eyes and not my own.

Easy to do? Probably not. Do I have to rely on my strength in order to accomplish true forgiveness? Definitely not! The problem lies with my choice. Either I believe what Jesus would have me to do, or I reject it. The verses following the Lord's Prayer in Matthew 6:9-13 state:

> "For if you forgive others for their transgressions, your heavenly Father will also forgive you. But if you do not forgive others, then your Father will not forgive your transgressions" (Verses 14-15 NASB).

And who are "our debtors"? Anyone and everyone whom we see as having wronged us. A family member who has acted in ways that were extremely hurtful. An ex-spouse. The business person who treats us badly. An annoying neighbor. A fellow Christian who is quick to point out our shortcomings while overlooking their own. Those who cause hurt to the people we love. Politicians. The list could go on and on and on, but forgiveness is required for each and every person on that list. "Lead us not into temptation, but deliver us from evil" surely includes the temptation to drag up old wrongs as well as holding grudges and harboring ill feelings.

There are times the Lord makes me face hard things and the day He taught me this was one of them. It is my hope that my experience will help others along the road on which we are all walking– the straight and narrow path that leads to life eternal. When I am dealing with someone who is my "debtor" I need to remember that my own forgiveness depends on how I treat the person involved in the situation. Certain people came to mind as I was praying, and there were others that popped into my head as I was writing this. Conviction can be quite uncomfortable until we are willing to say to God "Your will be done." We shall then resist temptation and be delivered from the evil of unforgiveness.

> "Pray, then, in this way:
> 'Our Father who is in heaven,
> Hallowed be Your name.
> Your kingdom come.
> Your will be done,
> On earth as it is in heaven.
> Give us this day our daily bread.
> And forgive us our debts, as we also have forgiven our debtors.
> And do not lead us into temptation, but deliver us from evil.
> [For Yours is the kingdom and the power and the glory forever.
> Amen']" (Matthew 6:9-13 NASB).

Day 76

YOU SHOULD HAVE KNOWN BETTER

My son Adam was supposed to wear a white or blue shirt to work at an electronics store - one with a button down collar. At first, it didn't matter if the shirt was a print, but then the "powers that be" mandated solid color ones. One day when Adam came home from work in his light blue shirt, I noticed that the T-shirt he chose to wear under it was not a plain white one. You could read through his dress shirt; on the front, in big black letters, was the word "Insight." The back letters were smaller than the ones in front, but still very visible. They read "Computers", "Hardware", and "Software."

I asked Adam if anyone had commented about his shirt situation – all he would tell me is, "Yes." Needless to say, I wanted to scream these words at Adam: "I taught you better than that!" Believe it or not, he should have known better. But I kept my temper in check and just moaned. I think I did say, "Oh, Adam! Why in the world did you do that?!"

I tried to explain to him that it is not very professional looking to wear printed T-shirts under his dress shirts, especially when you can read them right through the outer shirt. I felt like whoever saw him wearing that combo must think that his mom had not taught him very well. I guess the most embarrassing part for me was the thought that his actions reflected badly on my parenting skills.

I wonder if God has ever wanted to yell at us: "I taught you better than that!" His Word is full of teachings that we either ignore or blatantly disobey. And our lack of obedience is a poor reflection on the Church as a whole. People look at us and say, "What is the difference in how believers act and how worldly people act?" Many times, they reject Christ's teachings because we have chosen to go against what we have been taught. When God sees their rejection, do you think He wants to ask us, "Why in the world did you do that?! You should have known better!"

Let's do all we can to ensure that people see Christ living through us instead of seeing us "doing our own thing" while claiming to be His followers.

> "Therefore be imitators of God, as beloved children; and walk in love, just as Christ also loved you, and gave Himself up for us, an offering and a sacrifice to God as a fragrant aroma. But immorality or any impurity or greed must not even be named among you, as is proper among saints; and there must be no filthiness and silly talk, or coarse jesting, which are not fitting, but rather giving of thanks" (Ephesians 5:1-4 NASB).

Day 77

STILL I REMEMBER …

Have you ever been still-hunting? During my freshman year in college (located in upper East Tennessee), some friends and I went on an overnight trip with some people we met at our church. Their family owned a cabin up in the mountains. Besides the people we were with, I was the only Tennessean in the bunch. The rest were from Illinois, Indiana, and Kansas. Upon being informed that there were remains of an old still located the woods within hiking distance of the cabin, the out-of-state people decided that they wanted to go and find the site. I must admit I wanted to go as well.

We were a jolly bunch as we set out. We were laughing and talking as we crunched through all the dead leaves on the way to our destination. When we got there, we could see pieces of the still hanging in the trees and lying all over the ground. We even found a glass jug that had been used for moonshine. One of the family members told us that the government had found the still a few years earlier and had proceeded to blow it up. But they also divulged that there was a working still somewhere near that same area. One of the girls in our group wanted to see if we could find it. However, we explained to her the difference between ignorance and stupidity.

As we began to make our way back to the road, we did not go back exactly the way that we came. I don't remember why, it could have been that someone thought they knew a different path. We were traipsing along rather noisily when all of a sudden we heard shots being fired. In our wanderings around we had come just a little too close to the working still. We began to run like crazy. When we got to the road, we were dismayed to find that there was a very steep bank before we could get to it. As frightened as we were, we just sat down on our bottoms and slid down it, dodging rocks and trees as best we could. After reaching the road, we ran down it for quite a ways before we decided we were safe.

There is definitely a lesson here! Sometimes we who are Christians like to get a little too close to temptation. We poke and prod at the shattered remains of sins that we feel we have blasted out of our lives. We think that because we have overcome certain things in our battle with sin that we are dead to them, but we soon find out how quickly they can return to haunt us when they get stirred up. I think we feel a sense of power over the enemy that becomes prideful and leads to our stumbling all over again. We are all tempted, but when God gives us a way out, and then we turn around and get close to it again, we find it harder and harder to get away from it. Sin is something to be avoided, not something that we get as close to as we can without falling into it.

> "So if you think you are standing firm, be careful that you don't fall! No temptation has overtaken you except what is common to mankind. And God is faithful; he will not let you be tempted beyond what you can bear. But when you are tempted, he will also provide a way out so that you can endure it" (1 Corinthians 10:12-13 NIV).

> "Stay away from every kind of evil" (1 Thessalonians 5:22 HCSB).

Day 78

ROAD SIGNS AND GUIDEPOSTS

While reading through the book of Jeremiah, I took note of this Scripture:

> "Set up road signs; put up guideposts. Take note of the highway, the road that you take" (Jeremiah 31:21a NIV).

This verse comes from a plea from the Lord to the people of Judah. He called for them to set up road marks along the route of their captivity so that when He brought them out of captivity they could find the way back to their homeland. God had no intention of leaving His people in bondage in a foreign country; however, they chose by default to go there. Jeremiah and other prophets had warned them to repent and turn back to God; they ignored the warning and reaped the consequences.

With the warnings of captivity by their enemies, God also foretold of their return to their homes. He knew that their hearts would turn back to Him and that they would cry out for Him to save them. "Just as I watched over them to uproot and tear down, and to overthrow, destroy and bring disaster, so I will watch over them to build and to plant" (Jeremiah 31:28 NIV) was God's promise to His people.

We, too, need to set up road signs and guideposts in our walk with the Lord. Then, when the way seems dark and our vision is foggy, the road signs will keep us on the highway headed homeward. We should imprint in our minds those times when we strongly feel the Lord's presence. Answered prayers, including times when God has said "No!" and we have later understood the reason. Emotional, spiritual, and/or physical healing. Awe at the beauty of creation. Being held tightly in the Father's arms through stressful moments. Worship: either corporate or individual. Times when we can't help but utter praise to our God through words or music. Times when we try to fathom the depths of the blessings God has poured out on us and realize that we cannot begin to do so. Times when we cannot sense His presence but look back and see that He was there all along. Even times when God disciplines us; after all, we are His children.

Guideposts and road signs give us a sense of direction in a world filled with things that pull us away from our journey towards home. Are yours in place?

> "'I will bring him near and he will come close to me –
> for who is he who will devote himself
> to be close to me?'
> declares the Lord.
> 'So you will be my people,
> and I will be your God'" (Jeremiah 30:21b-22 NIV).

Day 79

CAT COOKIES

I must tell you that I thought twice about the subject of this devotion – it is not very appealing. However, I decided to write it anyway.

We used to have a dog named Nika, who had a disgusting habit. She loved what we refer to as "cat cookies". She searched the yard for where the cats had pottied to find these "treats". When someone did not get the lid tightly on the trashcan, Nika overturned it and scattered out all the bags of scooped-out cat litter that she found. It was an awful mess; however, she found a lot of what she was looking for.

Why in the world Nika thought the "cookies" were a treat, I will never know. Just the thought of her eating them turns my stomach. We fed her a premium dog food, so I don't think there was anything lacking in her diet. She just found joy in eating inappropriate snacks.

That thought leads to my application. How many "snacks" do we enjoy that are inappropriate for the Christian life? Unfortunately, the world has a lot of them to offer us; we are called "prudes" or "narrow-minded" if we refuse to indulge ourselves. Unwilling to appear weak in the eyes of those who partake of these snacks and consider themselves to be unaffected by them, we swallow our scruples and snack away. We ignore the nudges from the Holy Spirit that tell us we are allowing ourselves to consume that which is unsuitable for a child of God.

Because we consider it our right to be entertained, much of our unfit snacking material comes from the entertainment industry. We get so caught up in television, movies, electronic games, and the Internet that we do not listen to the voice of the Spirit of God. We don't heed when He warns us that our indulgences have negative nutritional value in our Christian walk. Impressing others by being able to join in conversations about a certain TV show or movie seems to matter more to us than making sure our minds are uncluttered and pure as possible. Our reading material can be another questionable source. So much that is available to us is not fit to read, including some literature that is considered classic. We bring a lot into our homes that we would never want to see lived out there. However, since it is called entertainment, we neglect to set a boundary line that we refuse to cross. One thing leads to another, and soon there is no shock value to what offended us in the first place. We become accustomed to what should be considered an insult to the Christian values to which we claim to adhere.

I guess the whole point I wish to make is this:

We all need to be more careful of what we are ingesting. God commands us to be pure and holy. That means we should beware of the "inappropriate snacks" we tend to devour without thinking twice about eating them. We should remember that we are to be setting an example to those who look to us for guidance. Just because we feel more "mature" than someone else does not give us an okay to indulge in "world cookies".

> "For I am the Lord your God. Consecrate yourselves therefore, and be holy; for I am holy" (Leviticus 11:44a NASB).

> "But immorality or any impurity or greed must not even be named among you, as is proper among saints; and there must be no filthiness and silly talk, or coarse jesting, which are not fitting … Therefore be careful how you walk, not as unwise men, but as wise, making the most of your time, because the days are evil. So then do not be foolish, but understand what the will of the Lord is" (Ephesians 5:3-4, 15-17 NASB).

> "Moreover, they shall teach My people the difference between the holy and the profane, and cause them to discern between the unclean and the clean" (Ezekiel 44:23 NASB).

Day 80

A GIFT FROM THE HEART

I have among my jewelry items a necklace. I have only worn it once or twice – and probably will never wear it again. However, this necklace is worth more to my mother-heart than other necklaces that I love to wear. Several years ago, my younger brother John was going through a phase where he loved to make necklaces and give them as gifts. While we were visiting at my mother's home, John let my son Jonathan design a necklace for me. Jonathan picked out special beads of various colors and sizes and strung them in a manner that he decided would please his mom. His face beamed with boyish pride as he handed me his carefully constructed gift. I remember thinking, "Oh, my!" One side of the necklace had skinny beads, and the other side had larger ones. There was no symmetry to the necklace at all; it was a conglomeration of beads on a string, complete with a barrel clasp. Of course, I thanked Jonathan profusely; but I wondered all the while if I could get him to restring it in a more eye-pleasing order. I stopped wondering when John told me how carefully Jonathan had worked to get his creation just right. When Jonathan was not around, the rest of my family teased me about the fact that I was going to have to wear the necklace so I would not hurt Jonathan's feelings.

Fast forward in time to a Sunday at our house. I was getting ready for church when Jonathan asked expectantly, "Are you going to wear the necklace I made for you?" How could I resist the hope on his face? I swallowed my pride and put it on. There were many comments made that day about my "interesting" necklace. "Jonathan made it for me!" I would reply. An understanding "Oh,

I see!" was the usual response. (I would imagine that people really wanted to say "Why in the world are you wearing such a strange looking strand of mismatched beads hanging around your neck?!" And I wanted to announce to people around me in general, "This is NOT my choice of jewelry!") My explanation made all the difference – everyone understood that a mother's pride bowed to the love of her son when I wore my necklace. It was his gift to me – a gift from his heart.

Many years ago, Our Father in Heaven sent us a gift from His heart– a gift in the form of a tiny baby. Babies are precious and wonderful; we consider them a blessing. The baby grew up, as babies do, and gave us another gift from the heart. However, this gift was not so "warm and fuzzy". It was grizzly and horrible: it involved pain and blood and agony and death. Definitely not something we would choose for ourselves. When we celebrate the birth of an infant Jesus, we don't enjoy looking into His face and remembering that there will be a crown of thorns shoved onto that very brow. When we see tiny hands reaching out of the manger bed, it is not pleasant to picture the nail scars that will eventually mar their perfection.

Christ's death, as well as His birth, is a gift from God's heart. The sacrifice of Jesus on the cross would not be our choice of a precious gift. However, God decided what the gift would be. Our choice is whether or not we will put on His gift. If we choose to wear it, there will be those who will ask, "Why in the world would you want to wear that?" They see God's gift as being outdated and irrelevant. When we put on Christ, human pride bows to Divine love as we wear God's most special gift– the one from His heart to ours.

"For God so loved the world, that He gave His only begotten Son, that whoever believes in Him shall not perish, but have eternal life. For God did not send the Son into the world to judge the world, but that the world might be saved through Him" John 3:16-17 NASB).

"Thanks be to God for His indescribable gift!" (2 Corinthians 9:15 NASB).

"You were all baptized into Christ, and so you were all clothed with Christ. This means that you are all children of God through faith in Christ Jesus" (Galatians 3:26-27 NCV).

Day 81

GRAN'S RULES

My dad taught my sisters and me how to play gin rummy. We never played it for money, just as a fun pastime. After I had learned the game from Dad, I used to play it with his mother. Playing cards with Gran was an interesting experience. She hated spreads (where you play three or four of a kind) because they could ruin a run (cards of the same suit in numerical order). And if the hand wasn't going her way, she would either bend the rules or change the way we played the game.

Our games with Gran used to have my cousin and me laughing so hard that our sides hurt. Strategy did not work very well; her games were never played the same way twice (unless she was winning). When you played cards with Gran, you never knew what you were doing for sure, as the rules could change at any time.

[Although I am going a certain direction with this devotion, I do have to say this. I spent many happy hours playing gin rummy with my grandmother. They involved a lot of hilarity and just plain good times that are a very pleasant memory. I would love to have the chance to play cards with her again and enjoy the love and camaraderie that we shared during runs and spreads and aces all over the table.]

We are living out the game of life. Every time we turn around, it seems like the rules change. What used to be the moral high ground is now politically incorrect. And things that were very wrong in days gone by are now considered okay. When someone exclaims, "That's bad!" they often mean, "That's very good!" It is no wonder that we are confused and frustrated as we muddle along trying to do the right thing, only to find out that it is becoming the wrong thing to do in our self-centered society. Today's saying seems to be "Rules are made to be broken." What was once considered sinful has now become a method of self-expression. Even in the church we find people willing to make "suggestions" out of commandments. Where there used to be dry ground we now find a sticky mud pit. However, if we look to the Creator of all things, we still find our feet planted on a firm path.

One thing in this life is for certain: Our God does not change. His rules for living do not change. We never have to worry about trying to keep up with new rules or new codes or new laws or new amendments because there aren't any nor will there ever be any. We know what He expects from us – holiness. We know what He promises us – eternal life. God deals with us where we are, helping us grow and learn and become what He has called us to be. But our growth and new awareness of Him and His work in our lives does not change Him. He remains the same Rock of Ages that He has always been. What changes is our perspective. The more we know Him, the more we realize how much more of Him there is to know. As we grow in our relationship with God, and we begin to comprehend how much He loves us, we realize that His rules are a comfort in that they are steadfast and sure.

When life seems to be an icky mess and your feet seem to be sliding out from under you, remember that God's unfailing love is rock solid under your feet and that His commandments are for your benefit. The standards will not be altered. If you stick with God's game plan, the rules will never change.

> "Every good thing given and every perfect gift is from above, coming down from the Father of lights, with whom there is no variation or shifting shadow. In the exercise of His will He brought us forth by the word of truth, so that we would be a kind of first fruits among His creatures" (James 1:17-18 NASB).

> "In the same way God, desiring even more to show to the heirs of the promise the unchangeableness of His purpose, interposed with an oath, so that by two unchangeable things in which it is

impossible for God to lie, we who have taken refuge would have strong encouragement to take hold of the hope set before us. This hope we have as an anchor of the soul, a hope both sure and steadfast" (Hebrews 6:17-19a NASB).

Day 82

OYSTER PIZZA

When my daughter Molly was about two months old, our family traveled from Indiana to Tennessee to visit my parents. It was one of the very few times that all six of their children managed to be in the same place at the same time. One of my sisters lived in North Carolina; another lived out of state as well. My youngest sister and brother were still living at home, and the older of my two brothers was there on leave from the Army. My husband Bob and I brought our three children; Terri brought her two, and Cindy and her husband had their daughter with them. All counted, there were ten adults and five children for meals. I am not counting Molly because she was still an infant. Bob and I, along with our children, were staying with my Aunt Betsy and Uncle Bill because there was not room at Mom's for all of us to stay there.

When it came time for dinner that night, my mother got one of her less-than-brilliant inspirations. Oyster pizza. And that is not the end of the story. After patting the pizza dough out onto a cookie sheet, Mom put oysters and tomato sauce on half of it. To avoid extra work in making dessert, she put pats of butter on the other half and sprinkled it with cinnamon and sugar. She was very pleased to have dinner and dessert all in one pan.

If the idea of oyster pizza makes you want to gag, just be glad you didn't have to look at it! Bob and I took one look at each other and decided that we needed to get back to Aunt Betsy's house. "Oh, but you'll miss dinner!" Mom declared. She didn't realize that that was the point. I have never liked oysters, and the thought of them on a pizza was more than repulsive. It didn't sit too well with Bob, either. We chose to obtain our supper from a restaurant on the way to my aunt's house.

There are days when we look at what life has to offer and long to say, "Yuck! I'll pass!" But that is not often possible. Our only choices are to deal with it or to hide our heads in the sand and hope it will go away while we aren't looking. The only trouble with hiding is that it usually gets worse while we are pretending it isn't there. So that leaves us shouldering burdens we don't want to bear and carrying crosses we don't want to carry. We grumble and complain that life is not fair, and we sigh, "If only ... " Our focus gets shifted from "How can I best serve God in this situation?" to "Woe is me!" In other words, we want to whine instead of shine. And we are not alone– just read the Old Testament for numerous examples of the whine perspective.

Sometimes we want to be selective. We will take part of what we are given, just not all of it. I would have probably eaten the dessert portion of Mom's pizza; after all, butter and sugar and cinnamon are usually pretty tasty on yeast dough. But those oysters on the other portion of it were disgusting, to put it mildly. However, in many life situations we don't have a choice to make.

The most wonderful part of life is that we do not have to go it alone. Jesus is there to shoulder the burdens and share in our disappointment. He comforts our grief, is a Friend in our loneliness, and He is the Light at the end of the tunnel of despair and depression. He never leaves us or forsakes us, even when we choose to ignore His presence and refuse His help. If you are looking at life right now, and you don't like what is there, turn to the One who can fill your plate with more many blessings than you can ask or imagine. What He has to offer will fill your soul with good things.

> "May the God of hope fill you with all joy and peace as you trust in him, so that you may overflow with hope by the power of the Holy Spirit" (Romans 15:13 NIV).

> "Be my rock of refuge,
> to which I can always go;
> give the command to save me,
> for you are my rock and my fortress" (Psalm 71:3 NIV).

"I remain confident of this:
I will see the goodness of the Lord
in the land of the living.
Wait for the Lord;
be strong and take heart
and wait for the Lord" (Psalm 27:13-14 NIV).

IN A PICKLE

I was glad when I finished up the last of my pickles for the year. The process was begun earlier that summer with cucumbers out of my garden. They were picked and scrubbed clean; then they went into a gallon-sized jar, where they were covered with a solution of vinegar, salt, pickling spices, and alum. After that, they sat in the jars for three months while they underwent a transformation from regular cucumbers to pickled ones. On the day after they were packed into the jars, I could already tell a difference in them. They had gone from bright green to a dull mossy color.

Finishing the process took place in November. I had to empty the cucumbers out of the jars and drain off all the liquid (one jar at a time). The jars got washed and dried for re-use in the next step of the procedure. As I sliced the cucumbers and put them back into the jars, my daughter covered each layer of slices with sugar. Each gallon jar got about seven cups of sugar. Now they had to sit for three days, and then they would be ready to eat. The sugar would draw moisture out of the cucumbers and dissolves in it, thus creating the pickle juice.

My mother-in-law gave me the recipe for these pickles a long time ago. She had gotten it from someone she knew; however, the recipe did not have a name. One day when I was at Quilters Guild, one of the ladies was talking about making pickles that had to sit in a jar for a long time before they were sugared. After inquiring about the solution she used, I discovered that she was making the same kind of pickles I had been. I asked if the pickles had a name and was told that they were called "Died and Gone to Heaven Pickles." The name must have come from the fact that they are very tasty; whenever I serve them, they get rave reviews.

While working on the tedious process of cutting up all those cucumbers, I began to compare the pickling process with the Christian life. It hit me that there could be another reason for the name of those pickles. Each person begins life as an infant. We grow and develop at different rates, but Christ is available to every one of us. When we accept him, we begin a transformation process that will go on for the rest of our earthly lives.

I scrubbed the cucumbers before the pickling process. In the same way, the blood of Jesus cleanses us from all unrighteousness when it is applied to our lives. The vinegar and salt in the pickling solution are preservatives. They alter the chemical nature of the cucumbers into something that will not spoil. The spices add flavor, and the alum makes them crisp. Our transformation involves preservatives as well. God works through the circumstances that we encounter every day to make us into what we ought to be. His Holy Spirit guides and directs us, providing the crispness we need to become more Christ-like. And the blessings that He pours out upon us constantly are the spices that give flavor to our lives. All this occurs while we live in this world. Even though we are surrounded by the unpleasant, God is able to change us from being "only human" into sons and daughters of Light.

Just as the pickles had to come out of the pickling solution to become a finished product, we will be taken out of this world to be made perfect. Whether we pass from this life before Christ's return or if we are called away by Gabriel's trumpet, we will enter a much better place. The old will pass away – when I removed the cucumbers from the jars, they did not look or smell the same as when I put them into the jars. (I refrained from tasting them; however, I am sure they did not taste the same either!) As for the sugar we poured over the pickles: sugar is known for its sweetness. And how sweet Heaven will be! Our transformation will be complete, and we will be in a place of no more sorrow, pain, or death. The process of becoming will be ended in a glorious reunion with loved ones who have gone on before, but best of all we will be with our Lord and Savior, who made our transformation possible.

"Therefore I urge you, brethren, by the mercies of God, to present your bodies a living and holy sacrifice, acceptable to God, which is your spiritual service of worship. And do not be conformed to this world, but be transformed by the renewing of your mind, so that you may prove what the will of God is, that which is good and acceptable and perfect" (Romans 12:1-2 NASB).

"For our citizenship is in heaven, from which also we eagerly wait for a Savior, the Lord Jesus Christ; who will transform the body of our humble state into conformity with the body of His glory, by the exertion of the power that He has even to subject all things to Himself" (Philippians 3:20-21 NASB).

Day 84

HAWK PRINT

Soon after we moved to the country, the strangest thing happened. My then teenage daughter Molly was in the living room, and I was in another part of the house – it was the middle of the afternoon. All of a sudden, there was a loud "BOOM!" and I heard the vibration of glass. Molly screamed. When I called out to ask her what had happened, she informed me that a bird had flown into the plate glass window and left blood on it. She looked out the window and saw a small dead bird lying below the window. Then she saw a hawk take off from the ground. Upon investigation, we realized that the small bird was not what hit the window. It was very stiff and had been dead already; besides that, the place where it was lying was not where it would have fallen had it been the one to smack against the window. The hawk left a telltale sign that it had been the culprit. We could see the print of its wings spread out, much like a fingerprint, and we could tell where its talons had hit. The small bloody spot was about the middle of its breastbone.

Molly and I speculated as to what had happened. We thought that maybe the hawk was after one of the white cats that live outside. One of them had been in the window earlier. She was on the ground when the hawk hit the window, and Molly said the cat was so scared she couldn't move. She just sat frozen in place with one paw in the air. Another theory we came up with was that the hawk saw one of the cats on the inside of the window and did not realize that there was glass was between it and the cat. However, we weren't quite sure if a hawk would view a cat as prey.

When I went outside to clean the window, I was fascinated by the "hawk print" that was there. I could see it much clearer from that perspective. I thought about leaving it for my husband to see, but I wanted to get the blood off the window. After wiping up the mess, I stepped back to see if I had managed to get the window clean. It was then that I realized what had probably happened. The window seemed like a big mirror. Instead of being able to look inside, all I could see was a reflection of the clouds, sky, and trees that were behind me. We decided that the hawk did not even realize there was anything there, it was just flying along and WHAM! There was something in its way that it did not expect in the least.

Life can deal us a blow much like that hawk experienced when it hit our plate glass window. We go sailing along, thinking everything is fine, and WHAM! Something hits us from out of nowhere. It might be the loss of a friend, family member, or a job. Perhaps it is the unexpected rebellion of a child or the sudden onset of a serious illness. The break-up of a marriage, job transfer, natural disaster – whatever it happens to be, we run into it with a loud BOOM! As we lie there stunned, we have to decide how we will deal with the problem.

Praise the Lord that we have a Savior who helps us get up and fly again. We may wobble a little (or maybe a lot), but using His strength we can carry on. After the first awkward attempts to get off the ground, the hawk flew away. It landed in a tree and rested there for a while, but soon it was soaring in the sky once again. Jesus gives us the ability to do the same thing in our lives. He gives us rest when we need it, and His power holds us up whenever we feel like we just can't get up and fly again. It is so wonderful to know that when we smack into a wall (or even a window!) our Lord is there with us through whatever trouble we face.

"Come to me, all who are weary and heavy-laden, and I will give you rest" (Matthew 11:28 NASB).

"Beloved, do not be surprised at the fiery ordeal among you, which comes upon you for your testing, as though some strange thing were happening to you: but to the degree that you share the sufferings of Christ, keep on rejoicing, so that also at the revelation of His glory, you may rejoice with exultation" (1 Peter 4:12-13 NASB).

Day 85

HERB GARDEN

I had an herb garden at the house where we used to live. In the spring, it would green up rapidly. I always enjoyed walking by it and smelling the mint and oregano and horehound and thyme and sage and tarragon. But there was a problem. New starts of oregano came up all over the place from where it went to seed the year before. If I was not careful, the oregano took over. The same thing was true with the spearmint, except it traveled underground as well as seeding. And the anise hyssop also popped up in some unexpected places. It became "thyme" (sorry, just felt a bit punny) to get out there and make sure everything stayed where it belongs. I also hoped there would be new starts of basil, as it is an annual and does not winter over. However, I could be sure that it would not come up in the right spot, and I would have to transplant it.

When I looked at the oregano that was trying to take over my herbs it brought to mind how some things can get too much of a hold on our lives. They can be good things (fresh oregano in spaghetti sauce – yum!), but they have progressed beyond their proper place. Maybe we enjoy a particular activity; however, if we are not careful it can take up too much of our time, effort and energy. Or perhaps we put more emphasis on it than our relationship with God and our families. We need to be careful that it doesn't become an idol to us.

Then there are things that pop up in unexpected places. Like pride. Pride that comes from knowing we are doing well and taking too much credit for ourselves. Pride that causes us to feel we can replace others that are meant to grow in that spot. Pride can be a good thing if it is centered in the right direction. I am proud to be a Christian, but the pride comes in belonging to Jesus. It is focused on Him, not me. I am proud to be used by God, and yet it humbles me that He is willing to call me His servant. I hope you understand what I mint. (Oops. The puns just keep popping out.)

Isn't it wonderful when things spring up in our lives that we didn't realize had been planted? Abundant joy in the midst of trials. Hope in the midst of desperation. Calm in the midst of a storm and light in the darkness. All gifts of our Heavenly Father! He knows just when we need to find those things in our lives. Thank You, Lord!

"May the grace of the Lord Jesus Christ, and the love of God, and the fellowship of the Holy Spirit be with you all" (2 Corinthians 13:14 NIV).

Day 86

I ALMOST SAID NO

Our house had been on the market for over a year. Our family was ready to leave a busy street corner and move to the country, but it seemed like no one else wanted to live on that busy corner, either. Needless to say, we were feeling quite discouraged.

One day during the middle of summer I was frantically preparing preschool crafts for Vacation Bible School. I had 120 carpenter aprons (preschool size) to be serged that day, among other things. The day for Adam and Molly (my son and daughter) to turn in their 4-H projects was rapidly approaching, and so we had that to deal with as well. We were also trying to catch up on the laundry that had piled up when Adam and Molly returned from a trip to Denver. Needless to say, the house was not in a very cleaned up state. When the phone rang that morning, I could only say, "Oh, please, Lord, don't let that be the realtor to show our house!" It wasn't. Then a few minutes later the phone rang again – the same prayer crossed my mind. But this time it was the realtor, and they did want to schedule a showing for that afternoon. Knowing that it would involve working double speed to get things ready, I almost said, "No, I'd rather not show the house today." In my mind, I could hear my husband telling me, "The only way to sell it is to show it!" so I reluctantly set an appointment for the showing.

During the time that the house had been on the market, I had tried my best to have it in very good shape whenever a showing was scheduled. Many times

I had neglected other things to get it ready, and no one came to look at it. And then there were all the reports back from the various realtors that showed it saying that their clients loved the house, they just hated the location. I guess all of this made such a bad impression on me that I determined I did not care. I would pick up as best I could and just let it go. Actually, I had a very negative attitude.

We usually left before the time people were supposed to arrive and then came back later. I decided that I was going to stay put and keep on working until someone showed up, especially since we had had a "no-show" earlier in that same week. When the people did come, I was almost ashamed to let them in because I knew all the things that still needed to be cleaned. Then Molly, Adam, and I left and went to the library so they could tour the house. Later that night, I told my husband that I did not think the people would even consider buying it. Imagine my surprise when our realtor called the next day to tell me that they had made an offer to purchase it!

There are times when the Lord calls us to do something. We look at ourselves and see all the imperfections and the stains and the clutter that we have gathered over the years. "Wait, Lord, I need to clean me up!" we tell Him. And His answer comes, "This job needs doing now." "But Lord, look at this mess! I can't help others when there is so much that needs to be taken care of in my own life." "If I could not use you I would not have asked," He replies. And so we reluctantly agree, wishing that we could just say no, but aware of the fact that God knows what we are and where we are in our lives. And the results can be amazing – just like it was amazing to me that those people bought our house even though it could have stood a thorough cleaning.

My personal testimony is this: God can use our imperfect lives to help others. There have been times that I wonder why I am writing devotions because I feel empty myself. But God pours out just enough inspiration for that moment, blessing me as much or more than anyone else. And so as long as He calls me to do so, I will keep on writing. What is He calling you to do?

> "For this reason since the day we heard about you, we have not stopped praying for you. We continually ask God to fill you with the knowledge of his will through all the wisdom and understanding that the Spirit gives, so that you may live a life worthy of the Lord and

please him in every way: bearing fruit in every good work, growing in the knowledge of God, being strengthened with all power according to his glorious might so that you may have great endurance and patience, and giving joyful thanks to the Father, who has qualified you to share in the inheritance of his holy people in the kingdom of light" (Colossians 1:9-12 NIV).

Day 87

WHAT I FOUND IN MY PURSE

I had been noticing that my purse seemed especially heavy. I picked it up one Wednesday morning and decided right there and then that I was going to discover why.

That particular purse is rather deep, with lots of compartments. When I carry it, I place my checkbook and wallet in a zippered pouch to keep them from getting lost in the bottom. I started doing that after I panicked a few times at the checkout line thinking my wallet was missing, only to find it hiding deep in one corner covered by a fold in the lining. There was nothing much in the main compartment besides my checkbook and wallet in their pouch.

There have been times that I manage to poke an item in my purse and then forget it is there. When I finally decide my purse has grown heavy, I will hunt through it to find out what is weighing it down. My Wednesday search began in the main compartment, as it tended to be the "holding place". I pulled out the pouch; all that was in it was my wallet and checkbook. I reached into one corner: nothing. I reached into the other corner and felt something cool and rather squishy. Suddenly, I felt rather squeamish, but I pulled out what I had found. The stench came right along with it– a rather large, and quite spoiled, yellow tomato.

I immediately knew what had happened. I had taken my neighbor shopping on the previous Wednesday. When we arrived back at her house, her husband gave me the tomato. I was busy helping her unload her items, so I set it on top of my purse because I did not want to forget it when I got home.

On the way home, the tomato jostled its way down into my purse, and I did forget about it. I was concentrating on unloading my groceries from the back of my minivan and getting things where they needed to go in the house. The tomato went out to dinner with me on Thursday evening. I think that is the first time I noticed my purse being so heavy. It went to church with me on Sunday and accompanied me to Sunday School following the church service. It was there when I went to lunch with a friend on Monday. It was not until Wednesday morning when I made an effort to locate my problem that I detected the by-now-disintegrating tomato.

Thankfully, nothing in my purse was ruined except a coupon that I did not want. It went in the trash with the tomato. However, the purse lining smelled horrible even after rinsing it off with water. By this time, I was ready to be done with the rotten tomato odor. I threw my purse and the pouch (minus my checkbook and wallet) into the washer with a load of clothes. Needless to say, I was very thankful it was not one of my good leather ones!

After I discovered the tomato in my purse, I began to think about the things we carry around in our lives that are out of place for a Christian. Buried grudges, bitterness, anger, jealousy, discontent, greed; the list could go on and on. We often forget they are there and wonder why our burdens seem so heavy and why things never seem to go right. We ask ourselves where God is instead of realizing we have weighed ourselves down with stuff that keeps us from sensing His presence in our lives.

I am happy to report that my purse survived its bath just fine. Even a stray mark from an ink pen came off in the wash. God is always ready to clean us up from the messes we make in our lives. My purse looked like new again. We can enjoy a welcome fresh-washed vitality when we allow God to cleanse us from our unrighteousness.

Sara Ray

I hear Jesus speaking: "Come to Me, all who are weary and heavy-laden, and I will give you rest. Take my yoke upon you and learn from Me, for I am gentle and humble in heart, and you will find rest for your souls. For My yoke is easy and My burden is light" (Matthew 11: 28-30 NASB).

Day 88

IS YOUR WOOD WET?

Have you ever listened to a rousing song or a compelling testimony and then heard someone say, "If that don't light your fire, your wood's wet!"? That phrase entered my mind when I had been preparing to teach a Sunday School lesson about Elijah and his triumph on Mt. Carmel. Elijah has always been one of my very favorite Old Testament characters, so I really "got into" the story. As He often does, the Lord brought out some things I had not considered before. And one of them had to do with wet wood.

If you know Elijah's story, you will recall that he had challenged 450 prophets of Baal and 400 prophets of Asherah to a contest. Two altars were to be built – one for Baal and one for the God of Israel. Wood was to be placed on top of the altar, as well as meat for a sacrifice. But no fire was to be placed on the altar. The prophets were to call down fire from Heaven. The god that answered was to be worshiped as the One True God. The prophets of the false gods spent hours calling him. They danced around the altar and finally began to cut themselves with swords to prove their devotion to him. However, no answer came. Now it was Elijah's turn. He built an altar with twelve stones, dug a trench around it, and placed wood on it. He laid the sacrifice on the wood, and then, instead of calling on the Lord for fire, Elijah commanded that four jars of water be poured over the wood and the sacrifice. After that had been accomplished, Elijah had them do it again and then again. Not only was the wood wet, the trench he dug was full of water as well.

We all know that wet wood is extremely hard to ignite, and you may not be able to get it to burn at all. Elijah's idea was to prove that it had to be divine intervention that would start a blaze on the altar. 1 Kings 18 tells us that when Elijah prayed, fire fell from Heaven and consumed the sacrifice, the wood, the stones, and even dried up all the water that was in the trench.

As I was contemplating the fact that Elijah soaked the wood with water in order to prove that God is the only God, the phrase about wet wood popped into my head. And I thought about the times when our "wood" is wet. Maybe we find ourselves depressed. Or maybe we are stressed out to the max. Or it could be that we have lost our joy in living because we are caught up in the humdrum of life. Whatever the situation, we cannot seem to get on fire for the Lord. We plod along, trying not to despair and feeling desperately sure that it will be hard for us to smolder, let alone be set ablaze. Hope seems to be one step ahead of us no matter how hard we try to catch up. But because we, too, know the God of Israel, we cry out to Him for fire from Heaven. And that is when we discover that the God of Heaven is the God of wet wood. He created it, and He can restore its capacity to burn.

So if your wood is wet, don't give up. God knows how to light a fire in the soggiest of places!

> "By awesome deeds You answer us in
> righteousness, O God of our salvation,
> You who are the trust of all the ends of
> the earth and of the farthest sea;
> Who establishes the mountains by His strength,
> Being girded with might;
> Who stills the roaring of the seas,
> The roaring of their waves,
> And the tumult of the peoples.
> They who dwell in the ends of the earth stand in awe of Your signs;
> You make the dawn and the sunset shout
> for joy" (Psalm 65:5-8 NASB).

Day 89

SPIRITUAL SPANKINGS

The book of Hebrews speaks about discipline. Why is it that we so often associate discipline with punishment? I guess it is because punishment helps us learn how to lead disciplined lives. It reminds me of a story about my son Jonathan and discipline; or should I say punishment?

When Jonathan was between the ages of two and three years old, he found himself in trouble. I don't remember what kind of trouble, just that it earned him a spanking from his mother. After his punishment, I plopped him down on his bottom. He sat there looking at me, with lower lip protruding and large crocodile tears rolling out of his eyes. Then he uttered the now-famous-in-our-family words: "Don't you fwip my buns again, you turkey!" Needless to say, I had to leave the room. I did not want him to see me laughing.

I wonder if God ever laughs at our reactions to his discipline. After all, we are His children and created in His image. If we as parents find humor in the ways our children deal with their punishments, can't you just picture our Heavenly Father chuckling with amusement at some of the things that He sees?

Jonathan was punished because he needed to learn that his actions were improper. We suffer consequences of the things we do wrong as well, but we love to make excuses for ourselves and give umpteen different reasons why we should not be punished ever again. We do not like to be disciplined, even though it makes us far better off in the long run.

As a parent, I have had to discipline myself to discipline my children. It would have been so easy to laugh at them and say, "Isn't that cute?" instead of taking care of the situation. What might be cute the first time becomes a bad habit if it is not dealt with. Over the years of raising my children, one of my heartfelt prayers was for wisdom to know how to discipline each one of them and for the strength and perseverance to use that wisdom.

God has the know-how to discipline us and the wisdom to do so in a proper manner. He uses many different things to ensure that we learn our lessons. I sometimes think He uses humor to lighten a distressing situation. Not to get us to laugh instead of cry, not to take the place of confession and repentance, but just to help us see that His love is surrounding us even when we need disciplined.

> "And have you completely forgotten this word of encouragement that
> addresses you as a father addresses his son? It says,
> 'My son, do not make light of the Lord's discipline,
> and do not lose heart when he rebukes you,
> because the Lord disciplines the one he loves,
> and he chastens everyone he accepts as his son.'

> Endure hardship as discipline; God is treating you as his children.
> For what children are not disciplined by their father? If you are not
> disciplined—and everyone undergoes discipline—then you are not
> legitimate, not true sons and daughters at all. Moreover, we have all
> had human fathers who disciplined us and we respected them for it.
> How much more should we submit to the Father of spirits and live!
> They disciplined us for a little while as they thought best; but God
> disciplines us for our good, in order that we may share in his holiness.
> No discipline seems pleasant at the time, but painful. Later on,
> however, it produces a harvest of righteousness and peace for those
> who have been trained by it" (Hebrews 12:5-11 NIV).

Day 90

SUNRISE

When my alarm went off one morning, it was still dark outside. My befogged brain did manage to remember that it was Sunday without thinking too hard. (It usually takes me a while to wake up.) My prayer to the Lord was that He would prepare my mind and heart for a day of worship. He answered my prayer in such an awesome manner that I was compelled to write about it.

Before the sun peeked above the horizon, a deep red blanket of light crept up the eastern sky. The clouds overhead began to glow in various shades of pink, ranging in color from a dark rose to a pale pastel. Then the sun burst forth in its brilliant red splendor. The clouds all the way from east to west reflected the sun's glory; each one was a masterpiece all by itself! Even looking out a west window, I could see the beauty of the sunrise. What a way to begin a day devoted to the worship and praise of an Almighty God!

As I stood in awe gazing at the clouds, I realized that the sunrise would not have been as breathtaking without them. My mind began to compare our lives to the beauty of the morning. Our humanness desires clear skies. We would like to sail through life in a carefree manner until the Lord calls us home, missing grief and pain, sacrifice and sorrow, opposition and persecution. We choose comfort over challenge. When clouds appear in our sky, we bemoan their presence. However, God uses those clouds in our lives to display His ability to see us through. Nonbelievers often see Christ in our lives (or *don't* see Christ) by our reactions to the hardships we face. When we rely on Him to get us through the difficulties, we cannot help but reflect His glory.

Each cloud took on a new beauty when it mirrored the sun. Each of us takes on new beauty when we mirror the Son. And just as none of the clouds are the same in the sky, none of us is the same as another. God has called us all to one purpose, but He uses us in different ways to fulfill that purpose. If one cloud is a deeper pink than another, it doesn't mean that the pastel cloud has any less of a place than the dark rose-colored one. It took all the clouds together to create the beauty of the sunrise.

"Great and mighty God, whose name is the Lord Almighty, great are your purposes and mighty are your deeds. Your eyes are open to the ways of all mankind; you reward each person according to their conduct and as their deeds deserve" (Jeremiah 32:18b-19 NIV).

"As for me, I will always have hope;
I will praise you more and more.
My mouth will tell of your righteous deeds,
of your saving acts all day long,
though I know not how to relate them all.
I will come and proclaim your mighty acts, Sovereign Lord;
I will proclaim your righteous deeds, yours alone.
Since my youth, God, you have taught me,
and to this day I declare your marvelous deeds.
Even when I am old and gray,
do not forsake me, my God,
till I declare your power to the next generation,
your mighty acts to all who are to come.
Your righteousness, God, reaches to the heavens,
you who have done great things.
Who is like you, God?" (Psalm 71:14-19 NIV).

Day 91

TEA TIME

If I could have only one beverage besides water, the choice would be easy for me to make. Tea. Hot or iced, it doesn't matter. And not the herbal stuff, either. I am also not very fond of instant; I like my tea brewed and fairly strong. I pour boiling water over the tea bag in my cup and set the timer on my stove for 2 minutes.

Some people do not care for strong tea. They pour water over the tea bag in their cup and remove the tea bag quickly, or even dunk the tea bag in the cup once or twice and call it good. Sometimes they will reuse the tea bag for another cup of tea.

As for me, I would rather have one cup of stronger tea than two cups of caramel-colored water. One thing is for sure, the longer the tea bag remains in the water, the stronger the tea becomes. There have been times that I have forgotten to take my tea bag out of my cup, and the tea gets so strong that it tastes bitter. Then I pour it down the drain and make a fresh cup. With a different tea bag, of course!

Studying the Bible can be like brewing tea. Sometimes people are in God's Word just long enough to produce a Christ-flavored existence, but not long enough for it to become a strong part of their lives. They find Scriptures that make them feel good but forget about the ones that call them to make changes in their life-styles.

Sara Ray

Then there are those that dig so hard in the Scriptures that they become nit-picky over minute details that are really unimportant in the grand scheme of things. They take things out of context and make mountains out of molehills, up to the point of causing divisions in their church congregation. Although they perceive themselves as strong in the faith, they create a lot of anger and bitterness.

If we keep our lives grounded in God's Word and use it to uplift others as well as ourselves, we are more like the cup of tea that is just right. Sweeten it with love and add the rich cream of God's mercy and grace. Then you will have something that will not only warm your life, but it will also bless the lives of those around you.

> "Your hands made me and formed me;
> give me understanding to learn your commands.
> May they who fear you rejoice when they see me,
> for I have put my hope in your word" (Psalm 119:73-74 NIV).

Day 92

ARE YOU LOOKING OVER A FOUR-LEAF CLOVER?

My dad was the king of four-leaf clover hunters. He could stroll across a lawn or park or even down a sidewalk during warm weather, and he would return with a mouthful of four-leaf clovers. I don't know why he stuck them there, but he would always pick the clovers very close to the ground, making sure they had the longest stem possible and put the end of the stem into the corner of his mouth. When he got home, the four-leaf clovers made their way into his books, pressed there for posterity. If I am looking through one of Dad's books even today, the chances are that I will find at least one clover.

My cousin Coleman once asked Dad how he found so many four-leaf clovers. Dad replied that he looked for the unusual. He didn't just stare at clover patches trying to find one with four leaves. He let his eyes roam over the patch until something looked different to him. After Coleman had received that information, Dad noticed him finding four-leaf clovers on his own.

Dad, one of his brothers, and their friend Roy used to travel to Oklahoma each May to attend a Christian men's gathering. My uncle and Roy decided to find out just how well Dad paid attention to where the clovers came from before sticking them into his mouth. They found a four-leaf clover and stuck it into a strategically located manure pile. Then they watched to see what Dad would do. Sure enough, when he spotted the clover, Dad "picked" it and into his mouth it went. He received lots of ribbing about that incident! I even heard the story repeated during the visitation before Dad's funeral.

Lesson 1: We often miss unique things in life because we are so busy looking at the obvious. Caught up in our day-to-day lives, we don't make the effort to find the extra-special moments that can mean so much in our album of memories. When we do find them, we hold onto them as long as possible, then stash them like keepsakes in the pages of our mental scrapbooks. As we observe other people, we forget to look for the unusual in them. We grow accustomed to viewing them in a certain way and don't look any further. There are many individuals who have unique gifts to offer, and we need to take the time to discover their special talents.

Lesson 2: Just like Dad did not look at the clover's manure pile surroundings, God doesn't look at the mire that surrounds us when He picks us out of the world and into His loving embrace. He sees us and not what is around us. He pulls us out of the world's filth and into His glorious light because He desires something far better for us than what we find ourselves encircled by. Thank You, Father, for Your grace!

> "Let us hold fast the confession of our hope without wavering, for He who promised is faithful; and let us consider how to stimulate one another to love and good deeds, not forsaking our own assembling together, as is the habit of some, but encouraging one another; and all the more, as you see the day drawing near" (Hebrews 10:23-25 NASB).

> "Now the God of peace, who brought up from the dead the great Shepherd of the sheep through the blood of the eternal covenant, even Jesus our Lord, equip you in every good thing to do His will, working in us that which is pleasing in His sight, through Jesus Christ, to whom be the glory forever and ever. Amen" (Hebrews 13:20-21 NASB).

Day 93

CLUMPING CAT LITTER

I prefer to use the type of cat litter that clumps when wet. When moisture hits the litter, the litter absorbs it and makes a ball, which can then be scooped out and thrown away. It has little effect on the rest of the litter in the box, especially if I scoop it before it has been there very long. However, if I miss a day, the other litter begins to absorb some of the moisture. This whole subject may seem disgusting, but I am using it to make a point.

Wouldn't it be wonderful if we could isolate our sins and temptations and throw them away? If they were in a nice neat little clump that we could scoop out and dispose of? That thought ran through my mind as I was working on litter box clean-out duty.

I also thought of the times I forgot to scoop for a couple of days. The clumps were still there, but they had softened and the litter surrounding them was damp. If we do not keep a diligent watch, we can find out that sin in our lives has taken hold and has begun to affect the way we live: our thoughts, our actions, and our relationships with others, much like the clean litter absorbing moisture from the clump. We are far better off if we recognize the sin or temptation for what it is before it begins leaching out into other parts of our lives. So keep your scoop handy ...

> "So I find this law at work: Although I want to do good, evil is right there with me. For in my inner being I delight in God's law; but I see

another law at work in me, waging war against the law of my mind and making me a prisoner of the law of sin at work within me. What a wretched man I am! Who will rescue me from this body that is subject to death? Thanks be to God, who delivers me through Jesus Christ our Lord!" (Romans 7:21-25 NIV).

Day 94

A MAIN INGREDIENT

Sometimes my family would grow tired of the same old things at meal times, so it is a good thing that I like to try new ways to prepare food. But one thing I have noticed is that, for the most part, I use the same ingredients over and over. There may be a few odd spice changes here and there; or perhaps a curious blend of ingredients that I would have probably not have come up with on my own. However, meat recipes have beef, chicken, turkey, pork, etc. And even though there are umpteen ways to cook potatoes, they have to be a main ingredient in a potato dish. The same thing applies to rice and pasta. So we are actually still eating the same things, they are just prepared in a different way.

A main ingredient in our walk with the Lord is the Word of God. It is food for our soul. It is always the same; it never changes. However, our lives do change. We face the challenge of new circumstances each and every passing day. No day is ever exactly like the one before it. So how can God's Word meet the needs of our lives when it never changes, and our lives do? Scripture tells us that "the word of God is living and active" (Hebrews 4:12 NASB). To our human minds, it seems impossible for printed words on a page to be alive, but we also know that all things are possible with God. It is up to us to make sure that God's Word is hidden in our hearts so that it is able to help us through any circumstance we face. And we do that by reading and studying our Bibles.

Scripture has a way of applying itself to where we are in life. It is beyond human comprehension, but God's Word never fails us. Verses that held no special meaning for us when we read through them at one point can suddenly become favorites as they help us deal with our current situations. As we diligently study our Bibles, God brings into prominence those things that help us through whatever we are facing at the time.

Let's all make sure that God's Word remains a main ingredient in our lives!

"Make me understand the way of Your precepts,
So I will meditate on Your wonders. ...
I have chosen the faithful way;
I have placed Your ordinances before me. ...
Teach me, O Lord, the way of Your statutes,
And I shall observe it to the end. ...
And I shall lift up my hands to Your commandments,
Which I love;
And I will meditate on Your statutes"
(Psalm 119:27, 30, 33, 48 NASB).

Day 95

FABRIC AND PATTERNS

Several years ago, my husband Bob had a class in North Carolina. It just happened to be in the same town where my sister Terri lived at the time, so I went with him. While he was in class, I spent time with Terri.

On one of our shopping expeditions, Terri and I went to a fabric store. We found a pattern that we both liked, so we hunted fabric to go with it. Then Terri came to my hotel room, and we began the process of making dresses. (Of course I took my sewing machine and serger!) Even though we were using the same pattern, our material looked totally different. Each of us liked both fabrics, but we agree that neither one of us would wear the print the other chose. Our remarks in the store had been, "I like that fabric, but it is not me."

God gives us all the same pattern: His Word. But we are not all cut out of the same fabric. Each one of us is uniquely gifted by our Creator. There are at least two lessons here. The first is that we shouldn't try to be someone that we are not. We cannot look at someone else and decide "That is how I would like to be." It is okay to be inspired by someone else's example, but we should never desire to be just like them. Their fabric would not look right on us.

Secondly, a pattern has to be put on the fabric following the grainlines. When I first started sewing, I would put the pattern pieces on the fabric as close together as possible. I thought the pattern people wasted a lot of fabric in their suggested layout. Needless to say, the garments I made did not hang right once they were put together, especially after washing them. What seemed like a waste of fabric really wasn't. As we follow God's pattern for our lives, we should remember that God knows what He is doing. Because He is the Designer, He knows how His pattern fits our fabric. When we try to change the layout, we cause problems.

If you are feeling disgruntled in life ask yourself these questions:
Am I trying to be someone I am not?
Have I let God fit the pattern on my fabric
or am I trying to do it myself?
The answers to them might give you a reason
why your life doesn't seem to fit you.

"Make me know Your ways, O Lord;
Teach me Your paths.
Lead me in Your truth and teach me,
For Your are the God of my salvation;
For You I wait all the day" (Psalm 25:4-5 NASB).

Day 96

EARS ARE FOR HEARING

When my son Adam was in kindergarten, the schools did routine hearing checks on the children. After receiving a paper saying that there was a problem with Adam's hearing, I scheduled an appointment for him with our family doctor. Upon examination, it turned out that Adam's ears were packed full of wax. When the doctor cleaned them, he jokingly told Adam that he shouldn't grow potatoes in his ears.

On the drive home, Adam turned the radio down. He fussed at all the rest of us for talking too loudly. Because the wax had been removed from his ears, his sense of hearing was a lot more acute than it had been for a long time. From then on, I knew that when Adam seemed to be losing his hearing, it was time to clean his ears. If they were really packed full, I needed to take him to the doctor to get the job done. (I do have to think that some of his lack of hearing when he became a teenager was intentional!)

There are times in our lives when we feel like we can't hear God's voice. I wonder if our spiritual ears are plugged up. We listen to so many other things that we become deaf to the still, small voice that we should hear above anything else. Keeping our ears open takes constant work. Sometimes it is just lack of effort on our part, and sometimes it is the lack of desire to hear God's voice that allows them to become closed to His whispers.

If you are trying to hear the Lord and His voice seems distant and muted, check your ears. It may be time for a clean out!

"He who has ears to hear, let him hear" (Matthew 11:15 NASB).

Day 97

BEAVER DAM

One November my husband Bob and I began to notice that the stream (drainage ditch) that borders our property was no longer flowing. The water in it kept getting deeper, and we could tell that it was stagnating; a film was forming on top of the water. Somewhere there was a problem. Bob walked through the field that lies across the road from us. There was still corn in it, so he could not get downstream far enough to see what was going on. I was concerned because I knew how fast that gentle stream can become a raging torrent when we have lots of rain. I also knew that it could overflow its banks and flood our drive.

I decided the best way to find out about the blockage was to telephone a county office but was unsure who to contact. After a couple of calls, I finally reached the right person. The man I spoke with assured me that he would have it checked out. The day before Thanksgiving, I received a return phone call. There was a large beaver dam across the ditch, plus an even larger one on the actual creek.

Several days later, they used a backhoe to knock a hole in the beaver dam. The owner of the property told me that we needed to keep an eye out for the same problem because beavers are known to rebuild their dams. Water began to flow through the stream again and the yucky stuff that was on the water disappeared. A couple of times since then it has rained pretty hard, and the water has risen to the top of the ditch; however, it stayed in its bounds. We were very thankful that the beaver dam was not blocking the water flow when we had the heavy rains.

As Christians, we experience such a blessing when the Holy Spirit is working in us and through us. It is a wonderful feeling to know we are being used by God for His purposes. Fresh joy flows through our lives as we are renewed and strengthened in our walk with Him. But sometimes things begin to block that flow of joy. Poor relationships with others, envy, lust, greed, selfishness, laziness, lack of focus; the list could go on and on. These "logs" build higher and higher until there is a dam across the stream that should be flowing in our hearts. What we once looked forward to becomes a drudgery— something that is expected to happen but not enjoyed. Church services are a habit, studying Scripture takes too much effort, and if we do utter prayers, they seem to bounce off the ceiling. A stagnant pool of misery and dissatisfaction forms in the place where joy once flowed so freely.

If you find yourself in this situation, it is time to take some drastic measures. First of all, earnestly desire for that dam to be broken. Cry out to God, asking Him to remove the blockage. Be willing to let go of the things that are keeping you from living within the will of God. Remember how blessed you felt when you were walking with Him, which makes it easier to loosen your grasp on the things that keep you from placing God where He needs to be in your life– #1. You may be shaken up a bit as the dam breaks loose, but trust me, it will be worth it!

> "I pray that the God of peace will give you every good thing you need so you can do what he wants. God raised from the dead our Lord Jesus, the Great Shepherd of the sheep, because of the blood of his death. His blood began the eternal agreement that God made with his people. I pray that God will do in us what pleases him, through Jesus Christ, and to him be glory forever and ever. Amen" (Hebrews 13:20-21 NCV).

> "Loving God means obeying his commands. And God's commands are not too hard for us, because everyone who is a child of God conquers the world. And this is the victory that conquers the world— our faith" (1 John 5:3-4 NCV).

Day 98

HELP! MY ROOF LEAKS!

My childhood years were quite interesting; I guess you can't say they were "normal." My parents bought a two-story house, moving there before I was very old; I have no recollection of the apartment we lived in prior to the move. It was our home until I had completed eighth grade.

Even though we had a second floor to our home, it was seldom used except for junk storage. There were three good-sized bedrooms up there, and another area that two twin-sized beds and a dresser would fit in. As more children joined our family, Mom and Dad just stuck more beds in the rooms downstairs.

One of the main reasons that we didn't use the upstairs was because the roof leaked. As time went on, the roof did not get repaired and the leaks grew worse and worse. By this time, my three sisters and I were sleeping in the living room; two of us on a three-quarter-size bed and the other two on cots that were pushed together to create a full-sized bed. The room above us had the leakiest roof in the house. We needed to keep water from coming into the living room. We placed a plastic rowboat in the center of the upstairs room, and then we took plastic sheeting and fastened it around the walls so that the plastic caught the drips and channeled the water down into the boat.

Our system worked well until the boat overflowed. If we forgot to check it during rainy weather, we would be awakened by drips coming down onto our beds. That meant that we had to get up, move our beds, go upstairs, open the window, and bail out the water. It always seemed that the boat filled up during the night!

This procedure became run-of-the-mill until we moved out of the house. Not long before we moved, I was walking across an area of the living room floor where there often had been a "drip-catcher"; it was so rotten that my leg went through the boards. Years of water damage and neglect had taken their toll. It was no wonder that the city where we lived finally condemned our house as unfit for human habitation.

I mean no disrespect to my parents, especially my father, but the truth of the matter is that they missed the boat. (Sorry, couldn't resist!) If the roof of the house had been repaired or replaced, the leaks could not have caused such extensive damage. I understand that there were times when money was an issue, but I also know that there were times when it wasn't. And wouldn't you think they would have learned a lesson from this situation? I must tell you that the house we moved to experienced the same fate in a few years– and all because of a leaky roof!

Have there ever been times in your life as a Christian that it seems like you just can't get it right? No matter how hard you try, you manage to feel like you're missing the mark. All it takes is a few clouds of doubt to hide the Son, some showers of gloom and self-pity to drip on what you feel to be hopeless anyway, and soon you are in a raging storm of despair and depression. You try to pray, but all you can hear is the drip, drip, drip of discouragement. You try to read God's Word, yet instead of finding answers to your problems, you manage to make yourself feel worse by comparing your own life to someone like Paul, who had learned to be content no matter what his situation. You find a few verses that make you feel better and use them for buckets to catch the drips, but still don't manage to come up with a solution to your problems. Stop and consider this: Maybe your roof is leaking! It could be that there are major issues you need to deal with that are keeping you from being what you could be for the Lord.

As for me, I know that there are times that I try to do a patch job on a roof that needs reshingling. Many of the issues that I find so frustrating are just symptoms of a problem that is farther-reaching than the situation at hand. The Lord has been helping me to realize that I have bitterness and unforgiveness that I need to relinquish, including forgiving myself for things He has already forgiven. There are things that I need to recognize as sin that I would rather ignore. He is also showing me that when I don't trust Him completely, I leave myself open to worry and frustration. And those openings leave room for drips of self-pity and feelings of worthlessness that are more than willing to follow a path of no resistance. He has been teaching me that if I am not careful, I will find myself with many more problems than a leaky roof. Not only does there seem to be a greater distance between Him and me, but my relationships with those around me are affected as well. If the real problem is not corrected, the list will only get longer.

God's advice to me, and to all who will listen to His voice, is to stop putting buckets under the drips and get the leaky roof fixed! And that doesn't mean patching it when it needs new decking and shingles. He is fully capable of doing the work. Our job is to let Him.

> "Give ear to my prayer, O God;
> And do not hide Yourself from my supplication.
> Give heed to me and answer me;
> I am restless in my complaint and am surely distracted …
> I would hasten to my place of refuge
> From the stormy wind and tempest …
> Cast your burden upon the Lord and He will sustain you;
> He will never allow the righteous to be
> shaken" (Psalm 55:1-2, 8, 22 NASB).

> "But as for me, my prayer is to You, O Lord, at an acceptable time;
> O God, in the greatness of Your lovingkindness,
> Answer me with Your saving truth.
> Deliver me from the mire and do not let me sink;
> May I be delivered from my foes and from the deep waters.
> May the flood of water not overflow me
> Nor the deep swallow me up,
> Nor the pit shut its mouth on me.
> Answer me, O Lord, for Your lovingkindness is good;
> According to the greatness of Your compassion, turn to me,
> And do not hide Your face from Your
> servant" (Psalm 69:13-17a NASB).

Day 99

PLASTIC WRAP

Life is full of great inventions. Plastic wrap has to be right up there among the top of the most used. Stop and think of all the things that you can do with it. For example, wrapping food items before placing them in the refrigerator or freezer. It can make a "lid" for bowls or jars that do not have one. It comes in handy for wrapping loaves of quick bread I am going to take to someone else. Many people use it in the microwave.

Plastic wrap works to help keep screws, bolts, nuts, and washers together with the item to which they belong. Industrial-sized wrap surrounds many items to be shipped. I could go on and on about the convenience of plastic wrap, and I am sure I would not cover all the ways people have discovered to utilize it. The ability of plastic wrap to cling to things is what makes it so useful.

There is a downside of plastic wrap: it likes to cling to itself. The very characteristic that makes it so helpful also can make it frustrating. It is annoying to be in the middle of wrapping something and have to stop and pull the plastic away from itself. If I am not careful when I tear it off the roll, the wrap clings to itself before I get it where it needs to go. Sometimes it is so stuck on itself that there is nothing to do but get a new piece and start over.

The Scriptures tell us that we should be like plastic wrap: we should cling to God.

Moses told the Israelites just before he died:

> "You shall follow the Lord your God and fear Him; and you shall keep His commandments, listen to His voice, serve Him and CLING to Him" (Deuteronomy 13:4*, emphasis mine).

Joshua, in his preparation for death, instructed the elders and other leaders of the people:

> "But you are to CLING to the Lord your God, as you have done to this day" (Joshua 23:8*, emphasis mine.).

If both of these great leaders of God's chosen people felt it was necessary to remind the Israelites to cling to God, it must have been important for them to do so.

In the Psalms, the David declares:

> "My soul CLINGS to You;
> Your right hand upholds me" (Psalm 63:8*, emphasis mine).

David, the man after God's own heart, recognized the value of clinging to God.

When plastic wrap is stretched over an object and clinging tightly, it is not very visible. Even colored wrap reveals the item it is surrounding. Our lives should be transparent enough so that people will see Christ living through us.

Romans 12:9* finds Paul admonishing believers:

> "Let love be without hypocrisy. Abhor what is evil; CLING to what is good" (emphasis mine). Jesus informed us in Luke 18:19* that "No one is good except God alone."

Maybe this is stretching, but here is my thought: we are told to cling to what is good, and we know that God alone is good; therefore, we should cling to God.

Sara Ray

Many of our problems lie in the fact that we choose to cling to ourselves instead of God. When asked to do something, our first thought is, "What's in it for me?" If we are called to sacrifice ourselves for the Lord's greater purpose, we cling even harder to our own wishes and desires. We consider our "rights" more important than the needs of others. Sometimes I wonder if some of the things we consider to be our "rights" are really "wrongs" in the eyes of a Savior who tells us, "You shall love your neighbor as yourself" (Matthew 19:19b*).

The ability to cling to what it is close to gives plastic wrap its usefulness. If we are closer to God than we are to ourselves, we will cling to Him, and He will enrich our lives so much that we will have no need to cling to ourselves. If we choose to cling to ourselves instead of to Him, we will be living a life that ignores God's greatest blessings and focuses on this world instead of the world to come.

*All Scripture references are from the NASB.

Day 100

MORE ON LAUGHTER

I once came across this statement: "When we are doubled over laughing, we are bending to keep from breaking." And I thought how true it is. A good dose of laughter can make tough situations tolerable. Maybe not easier, just bearable. It's like the old truism about laughing to keep from crying. We can always rejoice because God is there in the midst of everything. And if we find something to tickle our funny bone it sure makes the gray skies look a lot brighter.

Picture this: It was a gorgeous fall afternoon in Eastern Tennessee. As was the Saturday custom, Mom had given all four of us girls a bath and washed our hair. I think one of the reasons Mom only washed our hair once a week was because I hated it so much. It was a chore just to get me in the tub if I knew she was going to scrub my head. I was very scared of getting my head under water, and she had no patience with it. To her, I was being defiant. I don't think she realized how afraid I was.

Mom had probably done laundry and fixed food for lunch and who knows what all else. Usually, Saturday baths were in the evening, but she must have decided to go ahead and get it over with early on this particular day. I remember that it was autumn because our neighbors had raked up all their leaves and had been burning them in the ditch in front of their house. I can't remember exactly how old I was, but it had to have been before I was in third grade because my brothers weren't born yet. Anyway, Mom was very relieved to have that job completed. Since it was a gorgeous day, she allowed us to go outside (as long as we didn't get dirty) while she fixed supper. My youngest sister was too little to go outside with us, but the other three of us went. We were determined to be good.

One thing I will always be thankful for about my mother is that she read to us. We loved to listen to her, and we would bring piles of books for her to read. One of our very favorites was a set of Bible story books. Acting out stories was another of our favorite pastimes. We decided to use our playtime to dramatize the one of the Bible stories.

Unfortunately for her, Mom had recently read us the story of Job. One or two of us ventured over into the neighbor's yard to get some ashes so that we could "repent" properly. We sneaked in and got the mop bucket to contain them. We sat in the ashes one at a time and "repented", sprinkling them all over our heads because we just knew that was what Job did.

My tired mother came outside around this time to call us in. Can you imagine the spectacle that met her eyes? Can you imagine how she felt when she saw it? Three blond heads were now black and gray. Three scrubbed and shining little "angels" were now black and filthy. "I thought I told you *not* to get dirty!" Mom said forcefully. (She always tried not to yell.) She noticed that my sister Cindy was crying. Streaks of pink showed through her blackened face. And one of us informed her that we were repenting just like Job did. We hadn't meant to get dirty.

It was then that Mom started laughing and crying all at the same time. Faced with more baths and supper to finish and everything else she had to do, it was almost more than she could take. But she realized that we had listened and learned from that Bible story, and she just couldn't bring herself to punish us for getting dirty. She had to laugh, or she would have broken down and sobbed.

Telling this story is funny to me now but it was only after I became a mother and dealt with similar situations that I really realized how my mother felt that day. And it makes me laugh even harder because I know that struggle between total exasperation and exhaustion and the realization that some things aren't worth getting so worked up over. Three girls learned a lesson from their mother that day, and I am so glad that she taught us to laugh in the midst of trials.

"A happy heart is like good medicine,
but a broken spirit drains your strength" (Proverbs 17:22 NCV).

Day 101

COMFORT FOOD

So many days are those "just warm enough that the furnace seldom runs and just cold enough that the house feels chilly". These are days when I pull out my soup recipes – recipes that are pretty much ignored through the warm summer months. When I get chilled "plumb through to the bone" soup is just the thing to warm me from the inside out. And there are so many recipes to use!

Soup is definitely a comfort food. It adds warmth to your body and gives strength to you bones. I can recall snowy days from my childhood when we would play outside until we were all but frozen solid. Mom would call us in for a lunch of slices of cheese toast served with steaming mugs of tomato soup. And I remember how wonderful it felt to wrap my hands around my mug and soak up the warmth. Somehow, I can't imagine life without soup to warm my chilly days.

A good bowl of soup may warm our bodies, but it is God's Word that warms and comforts our souls. I can't tell you how many times I have been in need of a "warm fuzzy" and the Lord has brought a certain passage of Scripture to my mind. Even though I have experienced Him at work too many times to count, I am still awed by His care and concern for me. It is wonderful to know that He uses the time I spend in His Word for my benefit. And I love the way a passage of Scripture that I have read over in the past suddenly has a new relevancy for where I am in life. I marvel at how God uses that Scripture to convict, comfort, or encourage me.

It is my hope that maybe one of the "Comfort Food" verses that I am placing at the end of this devotion may become your "Soup of the Day"!

"For thus the Lord God, the Holy One of Israel, has said,
'In repentance and rest you will be saved,
In quietness and trust is your strength.' ...
Therefore the Lord longs to be gracious to you,
And therefore He waits on high to have compassion on you.
For the Lord is a God of justice;
How blessed are all those who long for
Him" (Isaiah 30:15a, 18 NASB).

"Your words were found and I ate them,
And Your words became for me a joy and the delight of my heart;
For I have been called by Your name,
O Lord God of hosts" (Jeremiah 15:16 NASB).

"If You, Lord, should mark iniquities,
O Lord, who could stand?
But there is forgiveness with You,
That You may be feared.
I wait for the Lord, my soul does wait,
And in His word do I hope" (Psalm 130:3-5 NASB)

"He heals the brokenhearted
And binds up their wounds.
He counts the number of the stars;
He gives names to all of them.
Great is our Lord and abundant in strength;
His understanding is infinite" (Psalm 147:3-5 NASB).

"Nevertheless I am continually with You;
You have taken hold of my right hand.
With Your counsel You will guide me,
And afterward receive me to glory.

Sara Ray

Whom have I in heaven but You?
And besides You, I desire nothing on earth.
My flesh and my heart may fail,
But God is the strength of my heart and my portion forever …
But as for me the nearness of God is my good;
I have made the Lord God my refuge,
That I may tell of all Your works" (Psalm 73:23-26, 28 NASB).

Day 102

TURBINE TROUBLE

I scheduled the annual maintenance check for our water softener the year after we moved to a country home. We had decided to get the extended service contract since our water was quite full of rust. I was hoping that the service man could program the softener so that we would not have to operate it manually. If one of us did not set it to recharge at least once a week, we would begin getting horrible rust stains on the bathroom fixtures, not to mention in the laundry. I had to use a special product in the white clothes to keep them from getting big yellow-orange blotches on them. Even though I kept increasing the hardness level on the softener, it never seemed to recharge on its own. It was supposed to regenerate on demand. We had been informed that the normal setting for this area is for 30 grains of hardness, but if there was a lot of rust that we might need to set it at 35. I had it all the way up to 55, and it was still not doing an adequate job.

The day the service man came, I explained to him the problem we were having. He was surprised to learn that the softener was not getting the iron out of the water, especially since we have an iron filter in the water line before it gets to the softener. The service man checked and cleaned most of the parts that were covered by the service agreement, and then he said that he needed to check the turbine. He asked me to turn on the hot water. I opened the tap in the downstairs bathroom and went back to the laundry area where he was working. After chatting with him a few minutes, I asked if he was done with the hot water. "You already turned it on?!" he exclaimed. I answered that yes,

I had turned the water on. The man then knew immediately where to locate the source of our problem.

There was a small turbine in the flow pipe of the water softener that turned when water is running through it. It was what let the electronic "brains" of the softener know how much water had been conditioned. After a set amount had flowed through it, the softener was supposed to set itself to regenerate that night. When the service man removed the turbine from the pipe, he discovered that the metal shaft in the center of it was bent. The bend kept the turbine from turning, thus causing the softener to "think" that no water had flowed through it. And it had been that way since it had been installed!

Now we knew why we had to set it manually for it to regenerate. The man replaced the turbine with a new one, revealing a bar graph we had never seen before. It blinked across the bottom of the screen on the control panel whenever the water flowed through the softener. The service man reset the hardness level to 35, and we had no more problems; although I must say that we sure went through a lot more salt pellets than we did before!

There are so many times in our lives that we get stuck in a rut and feel down and depressed. We don't feel the Lord at work in our lives because we are too busy feeling sorry for ourselves, or we are trying too hard to be what everyone else expects us to be. Maybe we are trying to be what we think God wants us to be instead of checking in with Him to see what He desires from us. We fail to register the work of God in our lives because our turbine shaft is bent. God may be working through us all the time we are bemoaning our lack of usefulness in His kingdom but because we are not looking for Him in the right places, we fail to discern His presence.

During times of spiritual renewal, it becomes much easier to identify the hand of God at work. Sometimes it is the sudden realization that God has been moving in the minute areas of our lives that spurs us toward a personal revival. As we begin to see Him on the job of providing for our needs and giving us direction for our lives, we become refreshed and feel the presence of His Spirit all the more. Instead of being drowned in waves of self-pity, doubt, and remorse, we join in the chorus of praise to the One that washes us clean from all unrighteousness and keeps us in the flow of those who are bound for the Promised Land.

When you are feeling depressed and lack the sense of the presence of God in your life, remember my water softener. Water was flowing through it even though the water softener was not registering the flow. Start looking for God in everything and you may be surprised just where you see His hand at work!

"And the Lord will continually guide you,
And satisfy your desire in scorched places,
And give strength to your bones;
And you will be like a watered garden,
And like a spring of water whose waters do
not fail" (Isaiah 58:11 NASB).

"It is You who has kept my soul from the pit of nothingness,
For you have cast all my sins behind Your
back" (Isaiah 38:17b NASB).

"And He will be the stability of your times,
A wealth of salvation, wisdom and knowledge;
The fear of the Lord is his treasure" (Isaiah 33:6 NASB).

Day 103

SONGS OF PRAISE

After taking a summer break, our choir would prepare to start rehearsals again. My husband Bob and I looked forward to it each year. We enjoyed singing praises to our Lord, and it was uplifting to join with others in doing so. Bob had a very good voice and could even sing solo, but I just sing. I can carry a tune well enough to stay in the choir, but that is about as far as it goes. However, I can be a small part of a large group of voices, and it takes many small parts to make a large whole.

One Sunday morning, while standing among the people in our congregation singing, I began to picture myself in a great throng of people in front of the throne of God. Every person was standing there singing praises to Him. Then all of a sudden I was standing there alone, pouring out my heart through my song to my Savior. He was listening to me, enjoying my praise to Him.

Some day we will be there – in front of God's throne – singing praises to Him. He will hear the whole multitude of His saints as we join our voices in a psalm of love to our Heavenly Father. We will be part of a whole – every voice blended perfectly in the most awesome human choir that has ever performed anywhere. But at the same time God hears the song of the great mass of people, He will also hear me. And He will hear you. Our voices will be blended together, yet He will distinguish my praise to Him and your praise to Him as well as every other person's praise to Him. That is the marvelous thing about our God. He can hear us all together at the same time He listens to a solo performance from each one of us. Mind-boggling, isn't it!

"Great is the Lord and most worthy of praise;
his greatness no one can fathom" (Psalm 145:3 NIV).

"Praise the Lord.
Sing to the Lord a new song,
his praise in the assembly of his faithful people" (Psalm 149:1 NIV).

Day 104

RIGHT WORDS

One of the reasons I love old hymns is that they bring back memories of my childhood, and I can "hear" loved ones singing along. Some of them I will never hear again in this life, but I will join them around God's throne, singing praises eternally. I hear my dad singing the bass parts you hardly hear anymore. I hear Gran as we sing "How Great Thou Art"; it was her favorite song. I hear Aunt Betsy's alto mingled with Uncle Bill's voice and know that they will sing together again someday. At times, I get all teary-eyed remembering.

And then there are the more humorous things caused by someone misunderstanding the words. One of the favorite stories my dad used to tell was one his father had told him. It seems that when my Poppy was little, he loved to sing and would belt out the songs in a loud voice. One Sunday his father was mortified as he sang out one of the verses of "Must Jesus Bear the Cross Alone." Instead of singing, "The consecrated cross I'll bear" he sang, "The constipated cross-eyed bear."

I also think of being the know-it-all oldest child and informing my one of my younger sisters that it wasn't bringing in the *cheese*, it was bringing in the *sheets*! (It was quite deflating to my ego to find out I was wrong as well. What in the world were *sheaves*?!!) I had a picture in my mind of all these women bringing in sheets off a giant clothesline. And then there was my cousin's favorite, "Praise Him, praise Him, tell of his elephant's greatness". I am not sure if that was really what he thought it said or if he made it up.

I'll never forget when I learned to read and realized that the song didn't say, "I stand amazed in the presence of Jesus the Tangerine." I can still picture the hymnal in my hands and the realization dawning in my brain that it was Nazarene instead of tangerine.

Reading opened up a whole new understanding. And that is how it works in our lives as we read and study God's Word. It explains and clarifies and gives a deeper comprehension, clearing up a lot of misconceptions. We can't just rely on what others say about the Bible because they may not have a good handle on it themselves. We need to read the right words for ourselves.

> "So we have the prophetic word made more sure, to which you do well to pay attention as to a lamp shining in a dark place, until the day dawns and the morning star arises in your hearts" (2 Peter 1:19 NASB).

Day 105

BLACK AND WHITE

Several years ago, I happened to walk through the living room just in time to see something quite curious. A chest sat in front of the picture window; it was just the height of the window sill. Our cats loved to lie there and bask in the sun, especially in the afternoon. They also enjoyed watching the birds that visited the bird feeder hanging on a branch not too far from the window. On this particular day, my son's cat Bash was the only one sitting on the chest. He was facing the window; sitting with his nose almost touching the glass. Except for a very few white hairs, Bash was solid black. On the outside of the window looking in was Onesimus, who was solid white. He was sitting in the same position that Bash was on the inside, facing him nose to nose. Because the two cats are approximately the same size, it seemed that one was an opposite reflection of the other one.

What a parallel to our lives! We are black with sin, but when God sees us through the blood of Jesus, we look white as snow. If we look at ourselves in a mirror, we may not particularly care for what we see, because the mirror shows us as we are. But if we view ourselves through the window of Jesus' blood, we see a soul that has been cleansed of all unrighteousness.

All too often we get depressed because we are looking in the mirror instead of through the window. We focus on the failures of our human nature instead of on our salvation through the blood of Jesus. Let's all make a conscious effort to see through the window to what Christ has done for us instead of looking in the mirror and bemoaning our sinful state.

"But if we walk in the Light as He Himself is in the Light, we have fellowship with one another, and the blood of Jesus His Son cleanses from all sin" (1 John 1:7 NASB).

"The blood of goats and bulls and the ashes of a heifer sprinkled on those who are ceremonially unclean sanctify them so that they are outwardly clean. How much more, then, will the blood of Christ, who through the eternal Spirit offered himself unblemished to God, cleanse our consciences from acts that lead to death, so that we may serve the living God!" (Hebrews 9:13-14 NIV).

Day 106

FLOWERS, WITH LOVE

Flowers seem to be the way to many a woman's heart. This is especially true for mothers. Who can resist the smiling face of a child holding out a fistful of dandelions or clovers?

My mother loved flowers, and one of her special favorites was violets. They grew in abundance around our yard and sometimes my sisters and I would have contests to see who could pick the most. Mom would be inundated with small purple blooms, which she would promptly put in water. With all four of us having picked violets, the vessel she placed them in had to have a fairly wide mouth to hold them all.

There would always be some that had stems that were too short to fit into the container without falling in. Mom had ways of dealing with that contingency – she showed us how to make a "picture garden". We would take a flat piece of glass into a shady corner of the yard. Mom would arrange the flowers, along with some greenery, to look like a picture and then she would cover it with the glass. The flowers drew moisture from the ground and stayed pretty for a long time.

Although Mom loved violets, she was also delighted with dandelion bouquets or any other offering from her children. She taught us how to take white clover flowers and make chains out of them. After that, she wore many a child-created clover necklace and even a tiara or two.

When I was junior-high age, my friend and I had a newspaper route. Part of that job included collecting money and then paying our bill every Saturday morning. We would ride our bikes down to the rendezvous point with our distributor, and then we had some time to do what we wanted before we rode home.

Not too far away from our Saturday destination was a florist shop. Alongside it there was a large dumpster, and my friend and I discovered that the dumpster held rejected flowers and ferns from the florist. Sometimes the only thing wrong with them was a discoloring – white or yellow carnations might have a splash of red. We started keeping an eye on the trash in the dumpster, and we were often rewarded with "nice" bouquets of flowers and greenery to take to our moms. Even though she knew where they came from, my mom was thrilled that I had taken time and effort to think of her. She displayed her flowers with the same pride that she would have if they had come from the florist.

The loveliest hothouse orchid would not have meant as much to my mother as a bunch of what many people would consider to be weeds, as long as they were given in love by one of her offspring. I remember many a fistful of yellow blooms brought to me by my children. I had to keep my flower containers on the porch due to allergies, but what counted with me was that my child had taken the time and the resources at hand to say in effect, "I love you, Mom! You are special to me! I am showing my love for you in this offering of flowers."

I wonder how many times I have failed to honor God by feeling that what I have to offer is inferior to what others give Him. He has placed me where I am, and if all I can give Him is a bouquet of dandelions, then He is just as blessed with them as He is with an offering of prize roses from a pristine garden. It is the act of giving Him what I have that counts. I can rest assured that He sees as much beauty in the dandelions as He does in the roses because He sees the love that comes along with them.

Just because someone else can offer what I consider to be a far superior gift than mine doesn't mean that God considers it that way. The problem would come if I could give roses and picked dandelions instead because I didn't want to offer my best. As long as I give Him my best, God honors the intent of my heart. And I should not hold back what I have to give because I think it is of lesser value that what someone else has to offer.

"Jesus sat near the Temple money box and watched the people put in their money. Many rich people gave large sums of money. Then a poor widow came and put in two small copper coins, which were only worth a few cents. Calling his followers to him, Jesus said, "I tell you the truth, this poor widow gave more than all those rich people. They gave only what they did not need. This woman is very poor, but she gave all she had; she gave all she had to live on" (Mark 12:41-44 NCV).

"God is the One who gives seed to the farmer and bread for food. He will give you all the seed you need and make it grow so there will be a great harvest from your goodness" (2 Corinthians 9:10 NCV).

Day 107

RUMBLE'S TREASURE

My granddaughter Maggie stayed nights at our house when her dad worked the midnight shift for a couple of years. My daughter (Maggie's mother), lived in a different state, and Maggie's dad was the custodial parent. Maggie wore pull-ups at night because she often wet the bed, and it was easier to change a pull-up than a soaked bed.

One morning I removed her wet pull-up and was planning on adding it to the outdoor trash can. I had the lid open, but just as I was in the process of dropping the pull-up into the garbage, one of our outdoor cats jumped up and grabbed it, thinking he had a real treat. This cat was named Rumble for two reasons: he purred very loudly, and he liked to "rumble" with other cats. The rest of our outdoor cats gathered around Rumble to try and share in his treat, but one whiff of it and they ignored him. Rumble ran down the sidewalk growling and smacking out with his paws. He wanted to make sure that no one had any ideas of sharing with him. Since I had no desire to have shreds of pull-up all over my yard, I followed Rumble down the sidewalk, laughing hysterically as I went. I informed Rumble that he really did not want what he had so labored to obtain, but he ignored me; after all, he was a *cat*.

Rumble finally stopped to check out his treasure. What a surprise he received, and not a pleasant one! Once he realized that he had captured a "potty" prize he left it on the sidewalk and ran away. I retrieved the pull-up and threw it in the trash. By this time, my sides were hurting from laughing so hard.

When it comes to life, I wonder how often we consider trash to be a treasure. We carry grudges and hard feelings for years because we are afraid if we let go of them we will lose something precious. We harbor bad tempers, bleak outlooks, and negative spirits because we think that is just who we are. We keep the Lord from pruning away the dead limbs of our lives, not realizing how much they are weighing us down and keeping us from growing spiritually. Like Rumble, we dare anyone, even God, try and take away our burden.

I hope this little story has brought a chuckle to your day! I also hope that it has made you stop and consider the things you hang onto that the Lord wants to remove for your own good. Life is too precious to waste it on vain treasures that are not treasures at all. God has so much more to fill our lives with if we would but let him do so!

> "I am the true vine, and My Father is the vinedresser. Every branch in Me that does not bear fruit, He takes away; and every branch that bears fruit, He prunes it so that it may bear more fruit" (John 15:1-2 NASB).

> "For this reason I bow my knees before the Father, from whom every family in heaven and on earth derives its name, that He would grant you, according to the riches of His glory, to be strengthened with power through His Spirit in the inner man, so that Christ may dwell in your hearts through faith; and that you, being rooted and grounded in love, may be able to comprehend with all the saints what is the breadth and length and height and depth, and to know the love of Christ which surpasses knowledge, that you may be filled up to all the fullness of God" (Ephesians 3:14-19 NASB).

Day 108

SEEKING TO SERVE

Only God knows what will happen in my future; my prayer is that He will fill it with joy – the joy of knowing Him, living for Him, and resting in His promise to take care of me. I pray that He will fill it with purpose – I want to live in His will, sense His presence, and be open and ready for His leading. I want to hear His still, small voice when He whispers to me. I want to see His hand at work in me and through me.

When God works through our lives, it brings joy indescribable. In the fall of 2009, I decided to use some yarn from my "stash" (those of you who quilt, sew, knit or crochet will know what I mean – you probably have a stash of your own). Our church congregation was having a special "Harvest of Talents". We were asked to donate things we had made. Those things would be sold at a silent auction at our annual Harvest Dinner, with the proceeds going to a mission. I decided to use the yarn to make a shawl to donate to that cause. I started working on it, but as the time came closer for the auction, I realized that I was not going to have it completed on time. I donated some crocheted dishcloths and net scrubbers instead.

I did not want to get discouraged and give up on the "Be a Friend Shawl", which was almost completed. I ended up not having quite enough of the "country rose" color yarn to finish it, so I trimmed it in white. I asked God what He wanted me to do with the shawl because I sensed that He had a purpose for it. Soon after my prayer, our neighbor Gerald went into the hospital. He was there for an extended period, and his faithful wife Anita was right there with him. I sensed that I should give the shawl to her. I knew her favorite color was pink, but the shawl was more of a mauve color, and I wondered if she would like it or not. Nevertheless, I followed that "still, small voice" inside me; the urging of the Holy Spirit telling me the shawl was for Anita.

Gerald was still in the hospital, and so I called his room and spoke with Anita. I asked her if she would like to go out to lunch with me the following day. She did, and I gave her the shawl on the way to the restaurant. I could hardly believe her reaction. She loved the color, and she informed me that she had wanted a wrap like that; however, she did not crochet or knit and could not figure out how to sew one. She was thrilled with my gift, especially when I told her that I had asked the Lord who it was for, and He had impressed upon me that it was hers. After our lunch, I dropped a very grateful Anita off at the hospital and drove home with tears in my eyes, marveling at how the Lord works in His mysterious ways. The timing, the color, the gift– all worked out perfectly. I even found the name of the color, "Country Rose" to be quite fitting since Anita's first name is "Rose" and she lives in the country!

As the future unfolds, let's keep our eyes open to see how God can use us, our ears open to hear His still, small voice, and our hearts open to obedience to Him.

> "We know that in everything God works for the good of those who love him. They are the people he called, because that was his plan" (Romans 8:28 NCV).

Day 109

AHA!

As I was reading Matthew's account of the man that has become known as the rich young ruler, I had one of those "Aha!" moments. I checked out the story in Mark and Luke, but neither of them mentions the part that struck me so profoundly.

In Matthew, when the young man asked Jesus what he had to do to get eternal life, Jesus told him that he should obey the commandments. The young man then asked which ones. Jesus replied, "Do not murder, do not commit adultery, do not steal, do not bear false witness, honor your father and your mother, and love your neighbor as yourself." (Matthew 19:18-19 HCSB) Here is the part that started my thought process: "love your neighbor as yourself". When I looked in Mark and Luke, that part was not included. Only Matthew, who wrote his gospel as an eyewitness account, mentioned it.

The rich young man felt like he had obeyed all the commandments that Jesus quoted to him, but had he really loved his neighbor as himself? The question that came to my mind as I was reading. Jesus knew his heart and knew that his wealth was very important to him. Even though the young man felt that he had kept the commandments, I wonder if he realized that he had failed in that one when Jesus told him to sell his possessions and give to the poor. Could part of the reason that he went away sad be that he recognized that his wealth meant more to him than his neighbor?

Sara Ray

This whole discovery got me to thinking about times in our lives when we think we are doing as the Lord commanded, yet we are somehow missing what He really wants us to do or what He wants us to be. I am in awe of how Scripture comes to life when we read and study it daily. I have read Matthew's account of the rich young ruler many times over, but it had never registered in my mind that "love your neighbor as yourself" was connected with this particular event. I just thank the Father for making His Word so fresh and vital in our lives.

> "For the word of God is living and active. Sharper than any double-edged sword, it penetrates even to dividing soul and spirit, joints and marrow; it judges the thoughts and attitudes of the heart. Nothing in all creation is hidden from God's sight. Everything is uncovered and laid bare before the eyes of him to whom we must give account" (Hebrews 4:12-13 NIV).

Day 110

STAINS

Stains are the bane of anyone who does laundry. Some stains will come right out with no care other than laundering. Other stains need to be pre-treated. Still others take more than one laundering to disappear. Then there are the stains that never come out, no matter how you treat them. A creative person can manage to cover them up with a little embellishment, depending on the garment and the location of the stain. But for some stains there is no hope. They will never come out, and they can't be covered up because they are too big or in a bad location on the garment. A favorite piece of clothing can be changed from a useful garment to either a "grubby" or a rag just because of a single stain.

Just as many things can stain our clothing, there are many things that can "stain" our walk with Christ. Sometimes all it takes is the realization that we are involved in something in which we should not be participating that gets our attention and stops us from doing it. Other times the Holy Spirit convicts us over a period of time until we finally come to the conclusion that whatever it is should be removed from our lives. And then there are the things that we try to hide from God's scrutiny. A little lace here or an applique there; embroidery or a decorative button somewhere else. The stain is covered up, but guess what? It's still there! We know it's there, and God knows it's there, and it is God that counts. Not family members that tell us what a neat idea it was to enhance our garment, nor friends who are envious of our creative ability; not even acquaintances that think we have it all together. Only the blood of Jesus can take away the stain and keep us from having to cover it up.

The best thing about God's cure for stained laundry is that there are no stains that Jesus' blood cannot remove. Our problem comes when we try to hide our stains from Him. We need to let go of our embellishing techniques and let the Master remove our guilty stains!

> "If we confess our sins, He is faithful and righteous to forgive us our sins and to cleanse us from all unrighteousness" (1 John 1:9 NASB).

Day 111

STONE SOUP

During the summer between my sophomore and junior years of high school my family experienced some very lean times. My dad was in a Veteran's hospital a few hours away from where we lived. My mom tried her best to find a job, but no one would hire her. She tried grocery stores and variety stores and restaurants just trying to find something, yet because she had her teaching degree they all told her she had too much education.

As a last resort, Mom tried to get welfare. Here again, she ran up against a brick wall because she was married. If she would divorce my dad, then she would have no problem getting assistance. Mom tried to explain that she only needed help to buy food for her six children until things got better, but it was of no use. She cried a lot during that summer. Every once in a while, someone would give us a few groceries, but never enough to last very long. One morning there was almost nothing left.

My three sisters and I had read the tale of stone soup several times over the years. It was a favorite of our two younger brothers. The story is about a hungry stranger who enters a town and manages to get the unwelcoming townspeople to furnish ingredients for a big pot of soup. We decided that we were going to put a rock in a pot of water and then have a prayer session and ask God to supply the rest of our stone soup. After having done so, we left it in His hands and went on about our business.

That afternoon, my sisters and I decided to go on a "hike" through our woods. We went up the hill to the railroad tracks and then made our way back down a different way, coming through an area where a man from our church had planted a garden that spring. After several weeks, he had neglected it; weeds had overtaken the vegetable plants. He finally told my mom that we could have whatever we could find in it, which wasn't much.

At one end of the former garden, ragweed grew quite tall. The ground was fairly soft, so the weeds pulled easily. I don't remember which one of us pulled up the first one, but we all joined in, yanking them up to create a path for us to get through. Then someone noticed that potatoes were falling out of the roots of the ragweed plants. The weeds had grown up where the man had planted his potatoes and when the potato plants died down, he could not tell where they were.

One of my sisters ran back to the house for a shovel and a wheelbarrow. We got several potatoes for our soup, as well as a few onions we found further down. Mom had come up with a soup bone from somewhere – perhaps from a neighbor. God had provided what we needed to make our soup, and we were extremely glad to have something to eat. We never dreamed that pulling weeds to make a path would yield something for our supper that night. Who would have ever dreamed that could happen? We had no idea that the man had planted potatoes and were definitely unaware of the spot where he had planted them. Our Father knew what we needed and supplied it in a most extraordinary way.

God has a way of answering prayers in ways that we could never think of ourselves. Next time you feel like you are up against a wall, just remember this story. If God gave us something so necessary out of something so useless (in our case it was ragweed), just think of what He can do for you. And don't try to figure out how He will answer. You probably can't.

> "With God's power working in us, God can do much, much more than anything we can ask or imagine. To him be glory in the church and in Christ Jesus for all time, forever and ever. Amen" (Ephesians 3:20-21 NCV).

> "And God is able to make every grace overflow to you, so that in every way, always having everything you need, you may excel in every good work" (2 Corinthians 9:8 HCSB).

Day 112

QUICK FRIED

I discovered a new "recipe" one day while preparing lunch. It goes something like this:

Heat a small amount of oil in a skillet on the stove while you are preparing salmon patties (or in my case, mackerel patties). Catch a glimpse of something floating down through the air. Hear the oil in your skillet sizzle. Look in the skillet and discover: Fried Spider!

All I could do was thank God (literally) that my fish patties were not in the oil and that I saw the spider drop down. It was the same color as the fish I was making into patties! I took a fork and removed the spider, then poured out the oil and started over.

Isn't that just like life? We never know what is going to show up on our "menu." We can plan all we want to; however, there always seems to be something unexpected. I just thank my God that He knows what we will be facing and that His strength and wisdom are ours to use if we will only reach out and accept them.

Withstanding the unexpected will strengthen our faith and help us grow in our walk with Christ if we learn from our experiences. Hopefully, we won't be like the spider and find ourselves quick fried!

"Consider it all joy, my brethren, when you encounter various trials, knowing that the testing of your faith produces endurance. And let endurance have its perfect result, so that you may be perfect and complete, lacking in nothing. But if any of you lacks wisdom, let him ask of God, who gives to all generously and without reproach, and it will be given to him." (James 1:2-5 NASB).

Day 113

SWEEPING IT CLEAN

Did you ever set out to do something and have it end up with the opposite outcome? We purchased a home that had hardwood floors. According to the sellers, the floors had all been refinished, which was true in a manner of speaking. The previous owner told us that one of the renters did the work. We soon decided that they started out in the living room and worked their way back through the house. By the time they reached the back bedroom, they finally learned how to remove the old finish and sand the floor before putting on the new finish.

Soon after our move, I decided that it was time to "find" my living room. It was over-crowded because it contained its own furniture, plus what would go in the basement family room. That space was in a "finish it up so we can use it" state. As I worked at moving furniture around, I had my broom handy to sweep up the dust that had collected under and around everything. My broom seemed to be making slow progress when I noticed something. The finish on the floor was so rough that it was sweeping the broom! Talk about working backwards; at that point I felt that I was getting further behind instead of making any progress. Wherever the broom had been, there were trails of clumped dust clinging to the rough finish on the floor.

When cleaning time comes in our spiritual lives, we often want to deal with the mess ourselves instead of letting God's Spirit rid us of the accumulated dust and dirt. Then we wonder why we feel that no progress is being made.

What we have ended up with is the same dust and dirt formed together in different clumps. We keep things we should discard and discard things we need to keep. Because we are human, we cannot grasp the ways of God. He deals with us in ways that we would have never imagined. We need to let Him do the sweeping so that we don't end up like I did in my living room when the floor was sweeping the broom!

"Have mercy on me, O God, according to your unfailing love;
according to your great compassion
blot out my transgressions.
Wash away all my iniquity
and cleanse me from my sin. ...
Create in me a pure heart, O God,
and renew a steadfast spirit within me" (Psalm 51:1-2, 10 NIV).

"But you were washed, you were sanctified, you were justified in the name of the Lord Jesus Christ and by the Spirit of our God" (1 Corinthians 6:11b NIV).

Day 114

TO RELY, WE MUST RE-LIE

Today you get a grammar lesson! Two words that are misused quite often are the verbs lie and lay. "Lie" is an intransitive verb, meaning that it has no receiver for its action, whereas lay is a transitive verb, requiring a receiver for its action. The problem with the two words comes because they have overlapping principal parts:

> Lie: lie, lying, lay, (have) lain
> He would rather lie down and nap than finish mowing.
> Nika is lying in the shade.
> The cat lay on our porch all afternoon.
> Her dirty clothes have lain on the floor for too long.
> Lay: lay, laying, laid, (have) laid
> Lay down that heavy rock before you drop it.
> (Rock receives the action of the verb.)
> The men were laying new carpet last night.
> (Carpet receives the action of the verb.)
> Bob and I laid the flooring in our family room.
> (Flooring receives the action of the verb.)
> Our clean clothes were laid on our beds for us to
> put away. (Clothes receive the action of
> the verb.)

Now that I have told you the proper usage of these two verbs and their principal parts, I am going to be bad and ignore the grammar lesson about which I have just informed you!

I just wanted to let you know that I know the proper usage before I use "lie" improperly; I know that "lay" is the proper word, but it will not produce the point I want to make, which is this:

To rely on God, we have to re-lie all of our burdens on Him and leave them there! (Somehow, re-lay sounds more like a race.)

How often do we give our problems to the Lord and then decide to pick them back up and worry over them awhile longer? I know that I am very guilty of doing just that! I stew and fret and wonder how in the world they are going to get solved while all the time God is patiently waiting for me to realize He can take care of them if I will put them back in His hands and *leave* them there. My Father in Heaven is able; I can depend on Him to take care of me. I just need to re-lie my burdens and rely on God.

> "For my iniquities are gone over my head;
> As a heavy burden they weigh too much for me" (Psalm 38:4 NASB).

> "Cast all your anxiety on him because he
> cares for you" (1 Peter 5:7 NIV).

> "Who is among you that fears the Lord,
> That obeys the voice of His servant,
> That walks in darkness and has no light?
> Let him trust in the name of the Lord and rely
> on his God" (Isaiah 50:10 NASB).

Day 115

SPICES

I sometimes make barbecue for lunch. My family loves the homemade kind. I begin by covering the meat with water, adding spices, and then simmering until the meat is tender. The flavorings I put in now will not make their way into the final product, but will be discarded. Bay leaves are one of my favorites. They give a wonderful flavor to the meat (they also add a lot to vegetable soup), but after the food is cooked, they are removed, along with the whole cloves. They add to the taste of my barbecue, but they are not meant to be a part of it.

As I was adding them, I began to think of my walk with the Lord. There are many things that add flavor along the way, yet they are not meant to be my food. Devotional books and thoughts are wonderful to read, but they should not be my source of nourishment. They can act as spices that bring out the flavor in many different ways, but my main focus needs to be on God's Word. I need to read it and study it and put it into practice. There is nothing wrong with reading the thoughts of others to enhance our Christian journey, but they can never replace the meat of the Bible. Spices and flavorings can never replace our source of nourishment.

"Establish Your word to Your servant,
As that which produces reverence for You" (Psalm 119:38 NASB).

Day 116

THE BEAUTY OF JESUS IN ME

I love the old chorus we used to sing entitled "Let the Beauty of Jesus Be Seen in Me". It is my prayer that others are able to see Jesus living in me. I very often ask the Lord that my life will be a reflection of Him, and it thrills me to no end when I am used to be the "hands and feet" of Jesus for someone else. It is all part of how the body of Christ works – we are to live in such a way that others sense Jesus in our lives.

A verse of Scripture I read one morning started a different line of thought; different but complementary. (Remember, there is a difference between "compliment" and "complement".)

What about me? When I look in the mirror do I see Jesus in me or do I cringe because all I can see is me? Have I let Him have full control or do I stifle that still, small voice within me that invites me to become more like Him and reflect His glory?

There are times when others may see Jesus in me, but I am painfully aware of my inadequacies and shortfalls. I know when I am "out of sync" with the Lord even though I can put on a good face to the world. I can say the right things and act the part of a dedicated Christian even when I am struggling on the inside. My words and my thoughts may go in two different directions. I can smile even though I am screaming on the inside.

So now the question becomes, "Do I want ME to see Jesus living in me?" Can I let go of who I want me to be for His greater glory? Will I let myself understand that His ways are higher than mine? Will I accept the fact that I am His creation, and He knows what is best?

Do I want to look in the mirror and see a person changed by His grace; one who is able to extend grace to those around me? Do I see someone forgiven who is willing to forgive? Does my reflection show me a person who is loved by the Almighty God, washed clean in the blood of the Lamb, adopted into the family of Christ, and filled with the Holy Spirit? Am I able to see the beauty of Jesus in me?

The next time I sing the old chorus, I need to include the person looking back at me from the mirror!

> "But we all, with unveiled face, beholding as in a mirror the glory of the Lord, are being transformed into the same image from glory to glory, just as from the Lord, the Spirit" (2 Corinthians 3:18 NASB).

Day 117

THE GREATEST GIFT

While reading the book of Exodus, I was drawn to verse 30 of chapter 32. A brief description of the prior verses: Moses had been on Mount Sinai for quite a while. God had presented him with the stone tablets containing the law. Meanwhile, the Israelites below grew weary of waiting and persuaded Moses' brother Aaron to make them a "god". Aaron formed the golden calf. God, who could see what was going on, grew very angry and declared His intention to destroy the people. Moses appealed for mercy and obtained it. He then went down the mountain, grew angry when he saw the actions of the Israelites, threw down the tablets and broke them. Moses then proceeded to mete out discipline to the people.

Next came Exodus 32:30: "On the next day Moses said to the people, "You yourselves have committed a great sin; and now I am going up to the Lord, PERHAPS I can make atonement for your sin." (NASB, emphasis mine.) Moses then proceeded to go back up the mountain and pleaded for mercy on the Israelite people once again.

As I read verse 30, a comparison came to my mind. Many years later there was another man that traveled up a hill to plead for mercy on behalf of sinful people. The difference between Moses and Jesus, other than the fact that Jesus was the Son of God, was this: Moses went with the idea that "perhaps" he would be able to make atonement for the sin of the people. Jesus climbed Calvary's hill with the assurance that He could make atonement for the sin of everyone. There was no doubt in the mind of Jesus that His sacrifice would accomplish exactly what He intended to do.

Jesus knew for sure that His willing sacrifice would atone for the sin of all mankind. He endured the limitations of human flesh and the bitter agony of being separated from His Father in order to give us the greatest gift of all: life with Him eternally.

"Thanks be to God for His gift that is too wonderful for words" (2 Corinthians 9:15 NCV).

"My dear children, I write this letter to you so you will not sin. But if anyone does sin, we have a helper in the presence of the Father— Jesus Christ, the One who does what is right. He died in our place to take away our sins, and not only our sins but the sins of all people" (1 John 2:1-2 NCV).

Day 118

ESTABLISHED FOOTPRINTS

Psalm 119 is full of verses that are very relevant to everyday living even in the 21st Century. Each time I read this psalm, I seem to find something else to highlight or scribble a note beside. God's Word is so very timely!

Not so very long ago I was impressed by verse 133:

"Establish my footsteps in Your word,
And do not let any iniquity have dominion over me" (NASB).

After pondering this verse, I wrote in the margin of my Bible, "Footsteps leave footprints." One frosty morning I read through this Psalm again, along with my earlier note, and recalled seeing my husband's footprints across the grass; he had left them there on his way to the shed to get his car to drive to work. I could tell where he placed each foot until the grass ended and the gravel began.

It is so neat how God works. Seeing Bob's footprints and reading this verse made me stop and think again about why I wrote the note in my margin. If our footsteps are established in God's word, we should leave footprints to prove it. For the past several years, I have decided to write notes on the pages of my Bible instead of in other places where I may or may not find them again. I highlight verses that speak to me as I read. Some verses are highlighted and underlined, meaning they have "jumped out" to me during different readings.

Psalm 119:133 is one of those verses, plus it has notes beside it. Besides the above mentioned, I have written, "This includes worry!" by the second part of the verse.

If someone picked up your Bible, could they see that your footsteps were established in God's word by the footprints you have left behind? I am not necessarily advocating that you have to write in your Bible; I know some people do not like to do so. However, if this is the case, you could write notes on separate paper and leave them between the pages, or keep a journal alongside your Bible. More importantly, is what we have learned from God's word evident in our lives? If not, we need to rearrange our priorities and leave some of those footprints so that we might:

> "Be diligent to present yourself approved to God as a workman who does not need to be ashamed, accurately handing the word of truth" (2 Timothy 2:15 NASB).

> "For whatever was written in earlier times was written for our instruction, so that through perseverance and the encouragement of the Scriptures we might have hope" (Romans 15:4 NASB).

Day 119

WHAT NEXT?

When my late husband Bob and I first started dating, his motto was: "Variety is the spice of life." After being around me for a while, he decided I had enough variety rolled into one package to suit him! He never knew what I would do next (for that matter, I don't either). I guess I come by it honestly because my parents were the same way. We never knew what they would do next.

The four girls at our house had our beds in the living room after my brothers were born; with two girls to a bed. My dad's recliner sat in one corner of the room, with bookshelves on either side of it and a floor lamp behind it. In the center of one side of the room, there was a fireplace and my mom's sewing machine sat in front of it. Our beds were in the opposite corner from Dad's chair, with the heads of them put together to form an "L" shape.

One night we were in bed and just about asleep when the lamp by Dad's chair came on. After a few seconds, it went back off. A few minutes later, it came back on again. By this time, we were wide awake. The lamp went back off. We started giggling. My dad came down the hall to see what was going on. He "checked out" the lamp, told us there was nothing wrong with it, and to be quiet and go to sleep. Then he went back to bed. The lamp came back on, and the laughter grew even louder. We could hear Dad coming back down the hall, but before he got there, the lamp went out again. This process repeated itself a couple of more times. Dad finally told us to get settled down and go to sleep. Enough was enough. The lamp did not come on again.

A few nights later, just when we reached the point of dozing off, my mom's sewing machine started running. It ran for several seconds and then shut off. We were instantly awake, having been primed by the prior lamp incident. Sure enough, we waited a couple of minutes and the sewing machine started running again. We decided to go and get Dad and tell him what was going on before he came to find out. He checked out the situation and then left, stating that sewing machines do not run by themselves. After he went back to bed, the machine came on again, ran for a bit, and turned off. My sisters and I were laughing so hard by this time that tears were streaming down our faces. Then we got really curious.

It finally dawned on us that maybe we should check things out for ourselves. When we did, we found out that the machine was plugged into another plug; this plug had a wire leading out of it. We followed the wire and it went into Mom and Dad's bedroom. It had an on/off switch on the other end. The sewing machine had a chair sitting next to it propped up against the knee pedal, which allowed the machine to run when Mom turned on the switch. She and Dad had been having a hard time not letting us hear them laughing!

Our Father God enjoys His children. He loves to surprise us with things that we could not have imagined; things that enrich our lives and cause us to rejoice in His overwhelming goodness and in the bountiful supply of His lovingkindness. He knows just the right touch that we need and He gives it at the perfect time. We can say along with David:

> "Praise the Lord, my soul;
> all my inmost being, praise his holy name.
> Praise the Lord, my soul,
> and forget not all his benefits –
> who forgives all your sins
> and heals all your diseases,
> who redeems your life from the pit
> and crowns you with love and compassion,
> who satisfies your desires with good things
> so that your youth is renewed like the eagle's" (Psalm 103:1-5 NIV).

Sara Ray

"I will sing to the Lord all my life;
I will sing praise to my God as long as I live.
May my meditation be pleasing to him,
as I rejoice in the Lord" (Psalm 104:33-34 NIV).

Day 120

A PRESSING ISSUE

Knowing I needed more exercise, I decided to "pump iron." In reality, it was because I needed to reduce congestion in my sewing area. There was a huge pile of clothing on my ironing board. Earlier in the year, I had been so proud of myself for ironing things as soon as they came out of the dryer. However, when the garden produce started, I did laundry in between all the chores associated with getting it picked and then canned, frozen, or dried. Needless to say, as long as an item wasn't necessary for someone to wear immediately, I just left it to be ironed at another time. Well, the time came for the task to be done.

I was able to further utilize my time at the ironing board by working on an embroidery project at the same time; all I had to do was change the thread when the machine was ready for a new color. (My sewing machine has an embroidery unit.) That was a good thing, because standing at the ironing board for quite some time is rather boring. Anyway, I thought the pile was never going to diminish. It was getting close to four o'clock in the afternoon when I decided I was going to finish the shirt I was working on and leave the rest for later.

The Lord has interesting ways of giving us encouragement to complete a task at hand – mine came in the form of a song. I had been listening to a Southern Gospel music radio station all day, and just as I was ironing what I considered to be the last shirt of the day the words to the song on the radio penetrated my thoughts: "Press on, press on ... " I finished the ironing.

There are days when it seems like everything we do is a never-ending chore. We work so hard to complete something just to find out that it is not quite finished. Yet we know the finishing process will take even more time, effort and energy. It would be easy to quit – to wait until later or to just give up entirely. That is when the Lord gently reminds us to press on. Keep going. Don't give up. Our task is not complete until we hear Him say, "Well done, thou good and faithful servant." And the awareness of His presence alongside us makes the satisfaction of a finished job all the more sweet.

> "Brethren, I do not regard myself as having laid hold of it yet; but one thing I do: forgetting what lies behind and reaching forward to what lies ahead, I PRESS ON toward the goal for the prize of the upward call of God in Christ Jesus" (Philippians 3:13-14 NASB).

(The emphasis is mine – needless to say, I had no trouble finding a Scripture for this devotion!)

AFTERWORD

It seemed fitting to end this book of daily devotions with the one that encourages us all to "Press on". When life gets discouraging, we all need the perseverance it takes to run the race and finish the course. The writer of Hebrews encourages that we "press on to maturity" (6:1 NASB). It is challenging when the Lord uses life's circumstances to help me mature in my faith.

My hope and prayer is that the thoughts in this book have somehow helped you in your journey towards our eternal home. It has long been my privilege to see the Lord at work in everyday things, and I love to be able to share with others the ways He helps me grow in my walk with Him as He continues planting Seeds of Light and Seeds of Joy!

ABOUT THE AUTHOR

Although she grew up in East Tennessee, Sara Ray now resides in rural central Indiana. She has written the popular "Cooks' Corner" column, which appears in her local newspaper, for nine years. Sara's family consists of her three children and their spouses, plus six grandchildren: three girls and three boys. She has four cats (three inside and one outside) and a Dachshund named Seigfried. Besides writing and cooking, Sara enjoys reading, sewing, and crocheting. Most of all, she is passionate about sharing the love of Jesus.

CPSIA information can be obtained at www.ICGtesting.com
Printed in the USA
LVOW06s0454251115

463907LV00004B/4/P